SIDE by SIDE

Extra

Book/eText/ Workbook 2A

- Expanded Grammar
- Self-Tests & Skill Checks
- Digital FunZone & Audio

Steven J. Molinsky • Bill Bliss

Illustrated by Richard E. Hill

Side by Side Extra Book/eText/Workbook 2A

Pearson Education, 10 Bank Street, White Plains, NY 10606

Staff credits: The people who make up the *Side by Side Extra* team, representing content creation, design, manufacturing, marketing, multimedia, project management, publishing, rights management, and testing are Pietro Alongi, Allen Ascher, Rhea Banker, Elizabeth Barker, Lisa Bayrasli, Elizabeth Carlson, Jennifer Castro, Tracey Munz Cataldo, Diane Cipollone, Aerin Csigay, Victoria Denkus, Dave Dickey, Daniel Dwyer, Wanda España, Oliva Fernandez, Warren Fischbach, Pam Fishman, Nancy Flaggman, Patrice Fraccio, Irene Frankel, Aliza Greenblatt, Lester Holmes, Leslie Johnson, Janet Johnston, Caroline Kasterine, Barry Katzen, Ray Keating, Renee Langan, Jaime Lieber, José Antonio Méndez, Julie Molnar, Alison Pei, Pamela Pia, Stuart Radcliffe, Jennifer Raspiller, Kriston Reinmuth, Mary Perrotta Rich, Tania Saiz-Sousa, Katherine Sullivan, Paula Van Ells, Kenneth Volcjak, Paula Williams, and Wendy Wolf.

Contributing authors: Laura English, Megan Ernst, Meredith Westfall

Text composition: TSI Graphics, Inc.

Illustrations: Richard E. Hill

Student book photo credits: Page v (computer) Oleksiy Mark/Fotolia, (tablet on left) Kuzmick/Fotolia, (tablet on right) Can Yesil/Fotolia; p. 27 (left) iofoto/Fotolia, (right) Doug Cannell/E+/Getty Images; p. 28 (top) Danita Delimont/Alamy, (middle) JOHN KOLESIDIS/Reuters/Corbis, (bottom) Eric Larrayadieu/Stone Sub/Getty Images; p. 59 (top) Bob Pardue – SC/Alamy, (middle top) John Foxx/Stockbyte/Getty Images, (middle bottom) Johnny Tran/Shutterstock, (bottom) Chad Ehlers/Alamy; p. 60 (top) the blue loft picture library/Alamy, (middle) Pep Roig/Alamy, (bottom) Fuse/Getty Images.

The authors gratefully acknowledge the contribution of Tina Carver in the development of the original *Side by Side* program.

ISBN-10: 0-13-246019-X
ISBN-13: 978-0-13-246019-4

Printed in the United States of America
2   18

CONTENTS

Introducing the *Side by Side Extra* eText!

The **eText version** of the Student Book offers *instant-access point-of-use audio* and serves as the student's virtual speaking-practice companion. Teachers can "flip" the lesson plan by moving some of the core conversation practice to students' time outside of class, thereby gaining back valuable instruction time for the multilevel expansion activities suggested in the Teacher's Guide, including games, discussion, brainstorming, and role-playing.

Welcome to the **FunZone**—a digital amusement park with attractions for each *Side by Side Extra* unit!

Stop by the *Picture Booth* for FlashCards practice and Picture/Word activities. *"Test Your Strength"* at our Vocabulary, Grammar, and Reading challenges. Step right up to the *Game Gallery* to play Concentration, Quiz Show, Crossword, and Lucky Letters games. Visit *ToonTown* for animation-based grammar activities. And don't miss the videos and music at the *ShowTime* stage.

The FunZone is optimized for computers and tablets. Students, BYOD—Bring Your Own Device.

1

Review of Tenses:
Simple Present
Present Continuous
Simple Past
Future: Going to

Like to
Time Expressions
Indirect Object
Pronouns

- **Describing Present,**
  Past, and Future
  Actions

- **Birthdays and Gifts**
- **Telling About**
  Friendships

VOCABULARY PREVIEW

Spring

Summer

Fall

Winter

1. Days of the Week
Sunday
Monday
Tuesday
Wednesday
Thursday
Friday
Saturday

2. Months of the Year

January	July
February	August
March	September
April	October
May	November
June	December

3. Seasons
spring
summer
fall/autumn
winter

What Do You Like to Do on the Weekend?

I We You They	} like to	
He She It	} likes to	eat.

A. What do you like to do on the weekend?

B. I like to read.

A. What does Ron like to do on the weekend?

B. He likes to go to the mall.

1. *Mr. and Mrs. Johnson?*
watch TV

2. *Tom?*
play basketball

3. *Sally?*
go to the beach

4. *you and your friends?*
chat online

5. *your grandmother?*
go hiking

6. *you?*

TALK ABOUT IT! *What Do They Like to Do?*

cook	play	swim	write
cooks	plays	swims	writes
cooked	played	swam	wrote
cooking	playing	swimming	writing

Robert likes to cook.
He cooks every day.
He cooked yesterday.
He's cooking right now.
He's going to cook tomorrow.
As you can see, Robert REALLY likes to cook.

Irene likes to play the piano.
She plays the piano every day.
She played the piano yesterday.
She's playing the piano right now.
She's going to play the piano tomorrow.
As you can see, Irene REALLY likes to play
    the piano.

Jimmy and Patty like to swim.*
They swim every day.
They swam yesterday.
They're swimming right now.
They're going to swim tomorrow.
As you can see, Jimmy and Patty REALLY
   like to swim.

Jonathan likes to write.
He writes every day.
He wrote yesterday.
He's writing right now.
He's going to write tomorrow.
As you can see, Jonathan REALLY likes to
   write.

Using these questions, talk about the people above with students in your class.

What does _____ like to do?
What does he/she do every day?
What did he/she do yesterday?
What's he/she doing right now?
What's he/she going to do tomorrow?

What do _____ like to do?
What do they do every day?
What did they do yesterday?
What are they doing right now?
What are they going to do tomorrow?

Then use these questions to talk about other people you know.

* swim – swam

Are You Going to Cook Spaghetti This Week?

A. Are you going to cook spaghetti this week?

B. No, I'm not. I cooked spaghetti LAST week, and
I don't like to cook spaghetti very often.

1. Are you going to watch videos today?

2. Are you going to drive downtown this weekend?

3. Is Mrs. Miller going to plant flowers this spring?

4. Is your father going to make pancakes this morning?

5. Are Mr. and Mrs. Jenkins going to the mall* this Saturday?

6. Are you and your friends going skiing this December?

7. Are you going to write letters tonight?

8. Is Dave going to clean his room this week?

9. Are you and your family going to WonderWorld this year?

10.

5. Are Mr. and Mrs. Jenkins going to the mall* this Saturday?

6. Are you and your friends going skiing this December?

7. Are you going to write letters tonight?

8. Is Dave going to clean his room this week?

9. Are you and your family going to WonderWorld this year?

10.

How to Say It!

Talking About Likes and Dislikes

Do you like spaghetti?
Yes, I do.

Do you like rock music?
No, I don't. But I like jazz.

Do you like to dance?
Yes, I do.

Do you like to ski?
No, I don't. But I like to skate.

Practice conversations with other students. Talk about things you like and don't like. Talk about things you like to do and don't like to do.

* going to the mall = going to go to the mall

5

What Are You Going to Give Your Wife?

| I'm going to give { my husband / my wife } a present. | I'm going to give { him / her } a present. |

A. What are you going to give your wife for her birthday?

B. I don't know. I can't give her a necklace. I gave her a necklace last year.

A. How about flowers?

B. No. I can't give her flowers. I gave her flowers two years ago.

A. Well, what are you going to give her?

B. I don't know. I really have to think about it.

A. What are you going to give your _____ for (his/her) birthday?

B. I don't know. I can't _____. I _____ last year.

A. How about _____?

B. No. I can't _____. I _____ two years ago.

A. Well, what are you going to give (him/her)?

B. I don't know. I really have to think about it.

1. *husband*
a watch
a briefcase

2. *girlfriend*
perfume
a bracelet

3. *boyfriend*
a jacket
a sweater

4. *grandmother*
flowers
candy

5. *daughter*
a bicycle
a doll

6.

What Did Your Parents Give You?

I	me
he	him
she	her
we	us
you	you
they	them

A. What did your parents give you for your birthday?

B. They gave me a CD player.

1. What did you give your parents for their anniversary?

a painting

2. What did Mr. Lee's grandchildren give him for his birthday?

a computer

3. What did your children give you and your wife for your anniversary?

a plant

4. I forget. What did you give me for my last birthday?

a purple blouse with pink polka dots

How to Read a Date

January 23rd	=	January twenty-third
November 16th	=	November sixteenth
December 31st	=	December thirty-first

A. When is your birthday?

B. My birthday is _____.

SIDE by SIDE JOURNAL

Write in your journal about your last birthday. What did you do on your birthday? Did your family or friends give you any presents? Write about it.

VERY GOOD FRIENDS: EAST AND WEST

Eric and Susan are very good friends. They grew up together, they went to high school together, and they went to college together. Now Eric lives in California, and Susan lives in New Jersey. Even though they live far apart, they're still very good friends.

They write to each other very often. He writes her letters about life on the West Coast, and she writes him letters about life on the East Coast. They never forget each other's birthday. Last year he sent* her some CDs, and she sent him a wallet. Eric and Susan help each other very often. Last year he lent* her money when she was in the hospital, and she gave him advice when he lost* his job.

Eric and Susan like each other very much. They were always very good friends, and they still are.

VERY GOOD FRIENDS: NORTH AND SOUTH

Carlos and Maria are our very good friends. For many years we went to church together, we took vacations together, and our children played together. Now Carlos and Maria live in Florida, and we still live here in Wisconsin. Even though we live far apart, we're still very good friends.

We communicate with each other very often on the Internet. We send them messages about life up north, and they send us messages about life down south. We never forget each others' anniversaries. Last year we sent them Wisconsin cheese, and they sent us Florida oranges. We also help each other very often. Last year we lent them money when they bought a new van, and they gave us advice when we sold* our house and moved into a condominium.

We like each other very much. We were always very good friends, and we still are.

* send – sent   lose – lost
    lend – lent   sell – sold

✔ READING CHECK-UP

TRUE OR FALSE?

1. Eric and Susan are in high school.
2. Eric lives on the West Coast.
3. Susan sent Eric some CDs last year.
4. Susan was sick last year.
5. They were friends when they were children.

6. Carlos and Maria don't live in Wisconsin now.
7. Florida is in the north.
8. Carlos and Maria send messages on the Internet.
9. Carlos and Maria moved into a condominium last year.

LISTENING

Listen and choose the correct answer.

1. a. I like to play tennis.
   b. I'm going to play tennis.
2. a. I went to the beach.
   b. I go to the beach.
3. a. Yesterday morning.
   b. Tomorrow afternoon.
4. a. I gave them a plant.
   b. I'm going to give them a plant.

5. a. We went to the mall.
   b. We're going to the mall.
6. a. They sent messages last week.
   b. They send messages every week.
7. a. He gave her flowers.
   b. She gave him flowers.
8. a. Last weekend.
   b. Tomorrow morning.

IN YOUR OWN WORDS

FOR WRITING AND DISCUSSION

A VERY GOOD FRIEND

Do you have a very good friend who lives far away? Tell about your friendship.

How do you know each other?
How do you communicate with each other?
  (Do you call? write? send e-mail messages?)
What do you talk about or write about?
Do you send each other presents?
Do you help each other? How?

PRONUNCIATION *Contrastive Stress*

Listen. Then say it.

I'm not going to clean my room this week.
I cleaned my room LAST week.

I'm not going to make pancakes this morning.
I made pancakes YESTERDAY morning.

Say it. Then listen.

I'm not going to watch videos tonight.
I watched videos LAST night.

I'm not going to write letters this evening.
I wrote letters YESTERDAY evening.

GRAMMAR FOCUS

SIMPLE PRESENT TENSE

I We You They	cook.
He She It	cooks.

LIKE TO

I We You They	like to/ don't like to	
He She It	likes to/ doesn't like to	cook.

PRESENT CONTINUOUS TENSE

(I am)	I'm	
(He is) (She is) (It is)	He's She's It's	cooking.
(We are) (You are) (They are)	We're You're They're	

SIMPLE PAST TENSE

I He She It We You They	cooked.

FUTURE: GOING TO

I'm He's She's It's We're You're They're	going to cook.

Am	I	
Is	he she it	going to cook?
Are	we you they	

	I	am.
Yes,	he she it	is.
	we you they	are.

	I'm	not.
No,	he she it	isn't.
	we you they	aren't.

INDIRECT OBJECT PRONOUNS

He gave	me him her it us you them	a present.

PAST TIME EXPRESSIONS

yesterday
yesterday morning / afternoon / evening
last night
last week / weekend / month / year
last Sunday / Monday /. . ./ Saturday
last January / February /. . ./ December
last spring / summer / fall (autumn) / winter

IRREGULAR VERBS

drive – drove
give – gave
go – went
lend – lent
lose – lost
sell – sold
send – sent
swim – swam
write – wrote

Complete each sentence with the correct form of the verb.

drive	give	go	watch	write

1. My parents are _____ TV in the living room. They _____ TV every evening.
2. I _____ my car downtown yesterday. I don't like to _____ downtown very often.
3. Monica likes to _____ letters. Last night she _____ a letter to her grandfather.
4. I'm not going to _____ my brother a tie for his birthday. I _____ him a tie last year.
5. My wife and I _____ swimming very often. We _____ swimming last weekend.

Match the questions and answers.

____ 6. What did your brother give you for your birthday?
____ 7. What did you give your brother for his birthday?
____ 8. What did your grandmother give your sister?
____ 9. What did your grandfather give your brother?
____ 10. What did you give your parents?
____ 11. What did your parents give you for your birthday?

a. She gave her a necklace.
b. They gave me a CD player.
c. I gave them a painting.
d. He gave me a watch.
e. He gave him a shirt.
f. I gave him a briefcase.

Count/Non-Count Nouns

- **Food**
- **Buying Food**
- **Being a Guest at Mealtime**
- **Describing Food Preferences**

VOCABULARY PREVIEW

1. apples	7. chicken	13. lettuce	19. pears
2. bananas	8. eggs	14. mayonnaise	20. pepper
3. bread	9. fish	15. meat	21. potatoes
4. cake	10. grapes	16. mustard	22. salt
5. carrots	11. ketchup	17. onions	23. soy sauce
6. cheese	12. lemons	18. oranges	24. tomatoes

Practice conversations with other students. Talk about the foods in this kitchen.

Make a List!

What are the foods in YOUR kitchen?
Where are they? Make a list.

12

Let's Make Sandwiches for Lunch!

1. Let's make pizza for lunch!
cheese

2. Let's make some fresh lemonade!
lemons

3. Let's make a salad for dinner!
lettuce

4. Let's make an omelet for breakfast!
eggs

5. Let's bake a cake for dessert!
flour

6. Let's make some fresh orange juice for breakfast!
oranges

7. Let's have french fries with our hamburgers!
potatoes

8. Let's have meatballs with our spaghetti!
meat

9.

How Much Milk Do You Want?

how much? too much	how many? too many
a little	a few

A. How much milk do you want?

B. Not too much. Just a little.

A. Okay. Here you are.

B. Thanks.

A. How many cookies do you want?

B. Not too many. Just a few.

A. Okay. Here you are.

B. Thanks.

1. *rice*

2. *french fries*

3. *ice cream*

4. *coffee*

5. *meatballs*

6.

Some of your friends are having dinner at your home. How do they like the food? Ask them.

A. How do you like the _____?

B. I think (it's/they're) delicious.

A. I'm glad you like (it/them). Would you care for some more?

B. Yes, please. But not (too much/too many). Just (a little/a few).
My doctor says that (too much/too many) _____ (is/are) bad for my health.

chocolate cake

cookies

ice cream

How to Say It!

Complimenting About Food

A. This *chicken* is delicious!*
B. I'm glad you like it.

A. These *potatoes* are delicious!*
B. I'm glad you like them.

* delicious / very good / excellent / wonderful / fantastic

Practice conversations with other students.

15

TWO BAGS OF GROCERIES

Henry is at the supermarket, and he's really upset. He just bought some groceries, and he can't believe he just spent* sixty dollars! He bought only a few oranges, a few apples, a little milk, a little ice cream, and a few eggs.

He also bought just a little coffee, a few onions, a few bananas, a little rice, a little cheese, and a few lemons. He didn't buy very much fish, he didn't buy very many grapes, and he didn't buy very much meat.

Henry just spent sixty dollars, but he's walking out of the supermarket with only two bags of groceries. No wonder he's upset!

* spend – spent

✓ READING *CHECK-UP*

Q & A

Using these models, make questions and answers based on the story.

A. How many *oranges* did he buy?
B. He bought only a few *oranges*.

A. How much *milk* did he buy?
B. He bought only a little *milk*.

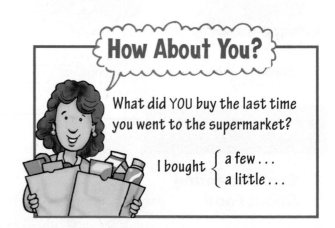

How About You?

What did YOU buy the last time you went to the supermarket?

I bought { a few ... a little ...

LISTENING

Listen and choose what the people are talking about.

1. a. cake	b. carrots	5. a. eggs	b. butter
2. a. fish	b. potatoes	6. a. rice	b. french fries
3. a. cookies	b. milk	7. a. oranges	b. salad
4. a. cheese	b. meatballs	8. a. lemonade	b. lemons

DELICIOUS!

Lucy likes french fries. In fact, she eats them all the time. Her friends often tell her that she eats too many french fries, but Lucy doesn't think so. She thinks they're delicious.

Fred likes ice cream. In fact, he eats it all the time. His doctor often tells him that he eats too much ice cream, but Fred doesn't think so. He thinks it's delicious.

TASTES TERRIBLE!

Daniel doesn't like vegetables. In fact, he never eats them. His parents often tell him that vegetables are good for him, but Daniel doesn't care. He thinks they taste terrible.

Alice doesn't like yogurt. In fact, she never eats it. Her children often tell her that yogurt is good for her, but Alice doesn't care. She thinks it tastes terrible.

ON YOUR OWN

Tell about foods you like.

What foods do you think are delicious?
How often do you eat them?
Are they good for you, or are they bad for you?

Tell about foods you don't like.

What foods do you think taste terrible?
How often do you eat them?
Are they good for you, or are they bad for you?

PRONUNCIATION Reduced *for*

Listen. Then say it.

Let's make a salad for dinner!

Let's make eggs for breakfast!

Would you care for some more cake?

It's bad for my health.

Say it. Then listen.

Let's make pizza for lunch!

Let's have ice cream for dessert!

Would you care for some more cookies?

They're bad for my health.

SIDE by SIDE JOURNAL

Write in your journal about your favorite foods. What are they? How often do you eat them? Why do you like them?

GRAMMAR FOCUS

Count / Non-Count Nouns

There isn't any	bread. lettuce. flour.

There aren't any	apples. eggs. lemons.

How much	milk cheese ice cream	do you want?
How many	cookies french fries meatballs	

Not too	much.
	many.

Just	a little.
	a few.

Choose the correct word.

1. We can't make a cake now.
   There (isn't   aren't) any flour.

2. There (isn't   aren't) any mayonnaise in the refrigerator.

3. We can't make an omelet.
   There (isn't   aren't) any eggs.

4. I don't want too (much   many) ice cream.
   Just a (little   few).

5. How (much   many) cake do you want?

6. I don't want too (much   many) cookies.
   Just a (little   few).

7. I bought just a (little   few) meat today.

8. My doctor often tells me that I eat too (much   many) desserts.

9. I bought a (little   few) carrots and a (little   few) cheese at the store.

10. How (much   many) rice did you buy?

11. I ate too (much   many) french fries!

Partitives
Count/Non-Count Nouns
Imperatives

- **Buying Food**
- **Describing Food**
- **Eating in a Restaurant**
- **Recipes**

VOCABULARY PREVIEW

1. a **can** of soup
2. a **jar** of jam
3. a **bottle** of ketchup
4. a **box** of cereal
5. a **bag** of flour
6. a **loaf** of white bread
7. two **loaves** of whole wheat bread
8. a **bunch** of bananas
9. a **head** of lettuce
10. a **dozen** eggs
11. a **pint** of ice cream
12. a **quart** of orange juice
13. a **gallon** of milk
14. a **pound** of meat
15. a **half pound** } of cheese
    half a pound }

Do We Need Anything from the Supermarket?

My Shopping List

a can of soup
a jar of jam
a bottle of ketchup
a box of cereal
a bag of flour
a loaf of white bread
2 loaves of whole wheat bread
a bunch of bananas
2 bunches of carrots

a head of lettuce
a dozen eggs

a pt.* of ice cream
a qt.* of orange juice
a gal.* of milk
a lb.* of meat
1/2 lb.* of cheese

* pt.	=	pint
qt.	=	quart
gal.	=	gallon
lb.	=	pound

A. Do we need anything from the supermarket?

B. Yes. We need a loaf of bread.

A. A loaf of bread?

B. Yes.

A. Anything else?

B. No. Just a loaf of bread.

1.

2.

3.

4.

5.

6.

7.

8.

9.

10.

Make a Shopping List!

What do you need from the supermarket? Make a shopping list.

How Much Does a Head of Lettuce Cost?

1¢	$.01	one cent	$1.00	one dollar
25¢	$.25	twenty-five cents	$10.00	ten dollars

A. How much does **a head of lettuce** cost?

B. **A dollar ninety-five.*** ($1.95)

A. A DOLLAR NINETY-FIVE?! That's a lot of money!

B. You're right. **Lettuce** is very expensive this week.

* $1.95 = { a dollar ninety-five
one dollar and ninety-five cents

A. How much does **a pound of apples** cost?

B. **Two eighty-nine.*** ($2.89)

A. TWO EIGHTY-NINE?! That's a lot of money!

B. You're right. **Apples** are very expensive this week.

* $2.89 = { two eighty-nine
two dollars and eighty-nine cents

1.

2.

3.

4.

5.

6.

7.

8.

READING

NOTHING TO EAT FOR DINNER

Joan got home late from work today, and she was very hungry. When she opened the refrigerator, she was upset. There was nothing to eat for dinner. Joan sat down and made a shopping list. She needed a head of lettuce, a bunch of carrots, a quart of milk, a dozen eggs, two pounds of tomatoes, half a pound of chicken, and a loaf of bread.

Joan rushed out of the house and drove to the supermarket. When she got there, she was very disappointed. There wasn't any lettuce. There weren't any carrots. There wasn't any milk. There weren't any eggs. There weren't any tomatoes. There wasn't any chicken, and there wasn't any bread.

Joan was tired and upset. In fact, she was so tired and upset that she lost her appetite, drove home, didn't have dinner, and went to bed.

✔ READING *CHECK-UP*

Q & A

Joan is at the supermarket. Using these models, create dialogs based on the story.

A. Excuse me. I'm looking for *a head of lettuce.*
B. Sorry. There isn't any more *lettuce.*
A. There isn't?
B. No, there isn't. Sorry.

A. Excuse me. I'm looking for *a bunch of carrots.*
B. Sorry. There aren't any more *carrots.*
A. There aren't?
B. No, there aren't. Sorry.

LISTENING

Listen and choose what the people are talking about.

1. a. chicken   b. milk
2. a. oranges   b. flour
3. a. cookies   b. bread
4. a. potatoes   b. lettuce

5. a. eggs   b. meat
6. a. cereal   b. bananas
7. a. cake   b. soup
8. a. onions   b. soda

What Would You Like?

A. What would you like **for dessert**?

B. I can't decide. What do you recommend?

A. I recommend our **chocolate ice cream**. Everybody says **it's** delicious.*

B. Okay. Please give me **a dish of chocolate ice cream**.

A. What would you like **for breakfast**?

B. I can't decide. What do you recommend?

A. I recommend our **scrambled eggs**. Everybody says **they're** out of this world.*

B. Okay. Please give me **an order of scrambled eggs**.

* delicious / very good / excellent / wonderful / fantastic / magnificent / out of this world

1. for lunch?
   a bowl of

2. for breakfast?
   an order of

3. for dessert?
   a piece of

4. to drink?
   a glass of

5. for dessert?
   a bowl of

6. to drink?
   a cup of

7. for dessert?
   a dish of

8.

How to Say It!

Making a Recommendation About Food

A. What do you recommend for *breakfast*?*

B. I { recommend / suggest } the *pancakes*.

* breakfast / lunch / dinner / dessert

Practice conversations with other students. Ask for and make recommendations.

Stanley's Favorite Recipes

Are you going to have a party soon? Do you want to cook something special? Stanley the chef recommends this recipe for VEGETABLE STEW. Everybody says it's fantastic!

1. Put **a little butter** into a saucepan.

2. Chop up **a few onions**.

3. Cut up (**a little/a few**) _____.

4. Pour in _____.

5. Slice _____.

6. Add _____.

7. Chop up _____.

8. Slice _____.

9. Add _____.

10. Cook for 3 hours.

When is your English teacher's birthday? Do you want to bake a special cake? Stanley the chef recommends this recipe for FRUITCAKE. Everybody says it's out of this world!

1. Put **a few cups of flour** into a mixing bowl.

2. Add **a little sugar**.

3. Slice (**a little/a few**) _____.

4. Cut up _____.

5. Pour in _____.

6. Add _____.

7. Chop up _____.

8. Add _____.

9. Mix in _____.

10. Bake for 45 minutes.

Project

Do you have a favorite recipe? Write the recipe, and share it with other students. Then as a class, put all your recipes together and make a class cookbook.

AT THE CONTINENTAL RESTAURANT

Yesterday was Sherman and Dorothy Johnson's thirty-fifth wedding anniversary. They went to the Continental Restaurant for dinner. This restaurant is a very special place for Sherman and Dorothy because they went there on their first date thirty-six years ago.

Sherman and Dorothy sat at a quiet romantic table in the corner. They looked at the menu, and then they ordered dinner. For an appetizer, Dorothy ordered a bowl of vegetable soup, and Sherman ordered a glass of tomato juice. For the main course, Dorothy ordered baked chicken with rice, and Sherman ordered broiled fish with potatoes. For dessert, Dorothy ordered a piece of apple pie, and Sherman ordered a bowl of strawberries.

Sherman and Dorothy enjoyed their dinner very much. The soup was delicious, and the tomato juice was fresh. The chicken was wonderful, and the rice was tasty. The fish was fantastic, and the potatoes were excellent. The apple pie was magnificent, and the strawberries were out of this world.

Sherman and Dorothy had a wonderful evening at the Continental Restaurant. It was a very special anniversary.

ROLE PLAY

Sherman and Dorothy are ordering dinner from their waiter or waitress. Using these lines to begin, work in groups of three and create a role play based on the story.

  A. Would you like to order now?
  B. Yes. For an appetizer, I'd like . . .
  C. And I'd like . . .

Now, the waiter or waitress is asking about the dinner. Using this model, continue your role play based on all the foods in the story.

  A. How (is / are) the _____?
  B. (It's / They're) _____.
  A. I'm glad you like (it / them).
     And how (is / are) the _____?
  C. (It's / They're) _____.
  A. I'm glad you like (it / them).

PRONUNCIATION *Of* Before Consonants and Vowels

Listen. Then say it.

a bowl of soup

a head of lettuce

a piece of apple pie

a bag of onions

Say it. Then listen.

a glass of milk

a jar of jam

a pound of oranges

a dish of ice cream

In your journal, write about a special meal you enjoyed—in your home, in someone else's home, or at a restaurant. What foods did you have? Who was at the meal? Why was it special?

GRAMMAR FOCUS

COUNT / NON-COUNT NOUNS

Lettuce Butter Milk	is	very expensive.
Apples Carrots Onions	are	

Add	a little	salt. sugar. honey.
	a few	potatoes. nuts. raisins.

IMPERATIVES

Please **give me** a dish of ice cream.
Put a little butter into a saucepan.
Cook for 3 hours.

Choose the correct word.

1. Add a (little   few) salt.
2. Cheese (is   are) very expensive this week.
3. Put a (little   few) cups of flour into a bowl.
4. There (isn't   aren't) any more lettuce.

5. Slice a (little   few) tomatoes.
6. The fish (was   were) tasty.
7. The potatoes (was   were) excellent.
8. Chop up a (little   few) nuts.

PARTITIVES

a **bag of** flour	a **dozen** eggs	a **jar of** jam	a **bowl of** chicken soup
a **bottle of** ketchup	a **gallon of** milk	a **loaf of** bread	a **cup of** hot chocolate
a **box of** cereal	a **half pound (half a pound) of**	a **pint of** ice cream	a **dish of** ice cream
a **bunch of** bananas	cheese	a **pound of** meat	a **glass of** milk
a **can of** soup	a **head of** lettuce	a **quart of** orange juice	an **order of** scrambled eggs
			a **piece of** apple pie

Complete the sentences.

9. I bought a _____ of lettuce.
10. Please get a _____ eggs.
11. We need two _____ of cereal.
12. I'm looking for a _____ of flour.

13. I had a _____ of chicken soup for lunch.
14. He had a _____ of pie for dessert.
15. Please give me an _____ of scrambled eggs.
16. I'd like a _____ of ice cream for dessert, please.

 26

Food Shopping

Everybody eats, and everybody shops for food!

In the past, people shopped for fruits, vegetables, bread, and meat at small food stores and at open markets. Before there were refrigerators, it was difficult to keep food fresh for a long time, so people shopped almost every day.

Life today is very different from the past. Refrigerators keep food fresh so people don't have to shop every day. People also have very busy lives. They have time to shop for food only once or twice a week.

People shop for food in different kinds of places—in small grocery stores, at large supermarkets, and sometimes at enormous wholesale stores that sell food and other items at very low prices. Some people even shop on the Internet. They order food online, and the company delivers it to their home. And in many places around the world, people still shop in little food stores and at open markets. There are certainly many different ways to shop for food these days!

FACT FILE

One Day's Food

Eggs: The world's hens produce more than 2 billion eggs a day—enough eggs to make an omelet the size of the island of Cyprus!

Chocolate: The world produces 8,818 tons of cocoa beans every day—enough to make 700 million chocolate bars!

Rice: The world produces 1.6 million tons of rice every day—an amount the size of Egypt's Great Pyramid!

Where People Shop for Food

People in different places shop for food in different ways.

These people shop for food at an open market.

This person buys a fresh loaf of bread every day at this bakery.

These people go to a big supermarket once a week.

Where do people shop for food in countries you know? Where do YOU shop for food?

Global Exchange

Glen25: Hi, Maria. How are you today? I just had breakfast. I had a glass of orange juice, a bowl of cereal, and a muffin. At 12 noon I'm going to have lunch. For lunch I usually have a sandwich and a glass of milk. Our family's big meal of the day is dinner. We usually eat at about 6 P.M. We usually have meat, chicken, or fish, rice or potatoes, and vegetables. How about you? When do you usually eat? What do you have? What's your big meal of the day?

MariaV: Hi, Glen. It's the middle of the afternoon here. Our family just had our big meal of the day. Today we had meat, potatoes, and vegetables. For breakfast I usually have a roll and a cup of hot chocolate. We don't have a big dinner in the evening. We usually have a snack early in the evening and a light supper at about 9:30.

Send a message to a keypal. Tell about the meals you eat.

LISTENING

Attention, Food Shoppers!

_d_	**1**	cereal	**a.**	$2.75
___	**2**	bread	**b.**	$ .40
___	**3**	orange juice	**c.**	$3.25
___	**4**	ice cream	**d.**	$3.49
___	**5**	bananas	**e.**	$1.79

What Are They Saying?

Future Tense: Will
Time Expressions
Might

- **Telling About the Future**
- **Probability**
- **Possibility**
- **Warnings**

VOCABULARY PREVIEW

Careful!

1. begin
2. end
3. arrive
4. return

5. grow up
6. get married
7. name
8. move

9. helmet
10. safety glasses
11. warning

Will the Train Arrive Soon?

(I will)	I'll
(He will)	He'll
(She will)	She'll
(It will)	It'll } work.
(We will)	We'll
(You will)	You'll
(They will)	They'll

Will he work?
Yes, he will.

A. Will the train arrive soon?

B. Yes, it will. It'll arrive in five minutes.

1. Will the game begin soon?
   at 7:00

2. Will Ms. Lopez return soon?
   in an hour

3. Will you be ready soon?
   in a few minutes

4. Will the guests be here soon?
   in half an hour

5. Will your brother get home soon?
   in a little while

6. Will you be back soon?
   in a week

7. Will the storm end soon?
   in a few hours

8. Will I get out of the hospital soon?
   in two or three days

What Do You Think?

| I / He / She / It / We / You / They | will work. |

| I / He / She / It / We / You / They | won't work. (will not) |

Do you think it'll rain tomorrow?

Maybe it will, and maybe it won't. We'll just have to wait and see.

1. Do you think Mr. Lee will give us a test tomorrow?

2. Do you think your daughter will get married soon?

3. Do you think your parents will move to Florida?

4. Do you think it'll be very cold this winter?

5. Do you think we'll have to work this weekend?

6. Do you think you'll be happy in your new neighborhood?

7. Do you think I'll be famous some day?

8. Do you think there will be many people at the beach tomorrow?

9. Do you think _____?

I CAN'T WAIT FOR SPRING TO COME!

I'm tired of winter. I'm tired of snow, I'm tired of cold weather, and I'm sick and tired of winter coats and boots! Just think! In a few more weeks it won't be winter any more. It'll be spring. The weather won't be cold. It'll be warm. It won't snow any more. It'll be sunny. I won't have to stay indoors any more. I'll go outside and play with my friends. We'll ride bicycles and play baseball again.

In a few more weeks our neighborhood won't look sad and gray any more. The flowers will bloom, and the trees will become green again. My family will spend more time outdoors. My father will work in the yard. He'll cut the grass and paint the fence. My mother will work in the yard, too. She'll buy new flowers and plant them in the garden. On weekends we won't just sit in the living room and watch TV. We'll go for walks in the park, and we'll have picnics on Sunday afternoons.

I can't wait for spring to come! Hurry, spring!

✔ READING CHECK-UP

TRUE, FALSE, OR MAYBE?

Answer True, False, or Maybe (if the answer isn't in the story).

1. It's spring.
2. The boy in the story likes to go outside during the spring.
3. The boy has a cold.
4. The trees are green now.
5. The park is near their house.
6. The boy plays baseball with his friends all year.
7. The family has a TV in their living room.
8. The boy's family doesn't like winter.

How About You?

What's your favorite season—spring? summer? fall? winter? Why? What's the weather like in your favorite season? What do you like to do?

They Really Can't Decide

I	
He	
She	
It	might clean it today.
We	
You	
They	

A. When are you going to clean your apartment?

B. I don't know. I might clean it today, or I might clean it next Saturday. I really can't decide.

A. Where are you going to go for your vacation?

B. We don't know. We might go to Mexico, or we might go to Japan. We really can't decide.

1. What's he going to make for dinner tonight?

2. What color is she going to paint her bedroom?

3. What are they going to name their new daughter?

4. When are you two going to get married?

5. What are you going to buy your brother for his birthday?

6. What are they going to do tonight?

7. How are you going to get to school tomorrow?

8. What's he going to name his new puppy?

9. What are you going to be when you grow up?

33

Careful!

A. Careful! Put on your helmet!

B. I'm sorry. What did you say?

A. Put on your helmet! You might hurt your head.

B. Oh. Thanks for the warning.

1. Put on your safety glasses!
   hurt your eyes

2. Don't stand there!
   get hit

3. Watch your step!
   fall

4. Don't touch that machine!
   get hurt

5. Don't touch those wires!
   get a shock

6.

How to Say It!

Asking for Repetition

A. *Careful! Watch your step!*

B. I'm sorry. { What did you say?
   Could you please repeat that?
   Could you say that again? }

Practice some conversations on this page again. Ask for repetition in different ways.

I'm Afraid I Might Drown

A. Would you like to go swimming with me?

B. No, I don't think so.

A. Why not?

B. I'm afraid I might drown.

A. Don't worry! You won't drown.

B. Are you sure?

A. I'm positive!

B. Okay. I'll go swimming with you.

1. *go skiing*
break my leg

2. *go to the beach*
get a sunburn

3. *go dancing*
step on your feet

4. *take a walk in the park*
catch a cold

5. *go to the movies*
fall asleep

6. *go to the company picnic*
have a terrible time

7. *go on the roller coaster*
get sick

8. *go sailing*
get seasick

9.

JUST IN CASE

Larry didn't go to work today, and he might not go to work tomorrow either. He might see his doctor instead. He's feeling absolutely terrible, and he thinks he might have the flu. Larry isn't positive, but he doesn't want to take any chances. He thinks it might be a good idea for him to see his doctor . . . just in case.

Mrs. Randall didn't go to the office today, and she might not go to the office tomorrow either. She might go to the doctor instead. She feels nauseous every morning, and she thinks she might be pregnant. Mrs. Randall isn't positive, but she doesn't want to take any chances. She thinks it might be a good idea for her to go to the doctor . . . just in case.

Tommy and Julie Harris didn't go to school today, and they might not go to school tomorrow either. They might stay home in bed instead. They have little red spots all over their arms and legs. Mr. and Mrs. Harris think their children might have the measles. They aren't positive, but they don't want to take any chances. They think it might be a good idea for Tommy and Julie to stay home in bed . . . just in case.

 ## READING *CHECK-UP*

CHOOSE

Larry is "calling in sick." Choose the correct words and then practice the conversation.

A. Hello. This is Larry Parker. I'm afraid I (might   can't)[1] come to work today. I think I (will   might)[2] have the flu.

B. That's too bad. (Are you   Will you)[3] going to see your doctor?

A. I think I (might   sure).[4]

B. (Not   Will)[5] you be at work tomorrow?

A. I'm not sure. I (might not   might)[6] go to work tomorrow either.

B. Well, I hope you feel better soon.

A. Thank you.

LISTENING

WHAT'S THE LINE?

Mrs. Harris (from the story on page 36) is calling Tommy and Julie's school. Listen and choose the correct lines.

1. a. Hello. This is Mrs. Harris.
   b. Hello. This is the Park Elementary School.
2. a. I can't.
   b. Tommy and Julie won't be in school today.
3. a. They might have the measles.
   b. Yes. This is their mother.
4. a. They aren't bad. They're just sick.
   b. Yes.
5. a. Thank you.
   b. It might be a good idea.

Good morning.
Park Elementary School.

WHAT'S THE WORD?

Listen and choose the word you hear.

1. a. can't   b. might
2. a. want to   b. won't
3. a. here   b. there
4. a. we'll   b. will
5. a. they'll   b. they
6. a. hurt   b. hit
7. a. I   b. I'll
8. a. red   b. wet
9. a. sick   b. seasick

Write a Note!

Your child didn't go to school yesterday. Write a note to the teacher and explain why.

........., 20......

Dear ....,

.... didn't go to school yesterday because

....

....

Sincerely,

....

PRONUNCIATION *Going to*

going to = gonna

Listen. Then say it.

When are you going to clean your room?

What color is she going to paint her bedroom?

How are they going to get to school?

Say it. Then listen.

When are you going to get married?

What's he going to name his cat?

When am I going to get out of the hospital?

SIDE by SIDE JOURNAL

Write in your journal about your future. Where do you think you might live? Where do you think you might work? What do you think might happen in your life?

FUTURE TENSE: WILL

(I will)	I'll	
(He will)	He'll	
(She will)	She'll	
(It will)	It'll	work.
(We will)	We'll	
(You will)	You'll	
(They will)	They'll	

I	
He	
She	
It	won't work.
We	
You	
They	

Will	I he she it we you they	arrive soon?

Yes,	I he she it we you they	will.

No,	I he she it we you they	won't.

TIME EXPRESSIONS

		days.
		minutes.
	a few	hours.
		weeks.
		months.
The train will arrive	in	a week.
		an hour.
		half an hour.
		a little while.
		two or three days.
	at seven o'clock.	

MIGHT

I He She It We You They	might clean it today.

Complete the sentences.

1. A. _____ Mrs. Sanchez return soon?

B. Yes, _____ _____. _____ return in an hour.

2. A. _____ the flowers bloom soon?

B. Yes, _____ _____. _____ bloom in a week.

3. A. _____ there be many people at the party tonight?

B. No, _____ _____.

4. A. _____ you call me today?

B. Yes, _____ _____. _____ call you soon.

5. A. _____ your brother be ready soon?

B. No, _____ _____. He's still sleeping.

6. A. _____ you and your wife visit us soon?

B. Yes, _____ _____. _____ visit you on Sunday.

7. A. Do you think it _____ be a nice day tomorrow?

B. Maybe _____ _____, and maybe _____ _____.

8. A. Do you think _____ catch a cold?

B. No, you _____. _____ be fine.

Comparatives
Should
Possessive Pronouns

- **Making Comparisons**
- **Advice**
- **Expressing Opinions**
- **Agreement and Disagreement**

VOCABULARY PREVIEW

1. cute	6. hospitable	11. polite
2. delicious	7. hot/spicy	12. powerful
3. exciting	8. intelligent/smart	13. soft
4. fashionable	9. lazy	14. talented
5. friendly	10. light	15. talkative

My New Bicycle Is Faster

soft – softer small – smaller	large – larger safe – safer	big – bigger hot – hotter	fancy – fancier pretty – prettier

A. I think you'll like my new bicycle.

B. But I liked your OLD bicycle. It was **fast**.

A. That's right. But my new bicycle is **faster**.

1. *rug*
   soft

2. *tennis racket*
   light

3. *apartment*
   large

4. *neighborhood*
   safe

5. *office*
   big

6. *recipe for chili*
   hot

7. *dog*
   friendly

8. *sports car*
   fancy

9. *dishwasher*
   quiet

10. *wig*
   pretty

11. *cell phone*
   small

12. *cat*
   cute

My New Rocking Chair Is More Comfortable

fast – faster nice – nicer big – bigger pretty – prettier	comfortable – more comfortable beautiful – more beautiful interesting – more interesting intelligent – more intelligent

A. I think you'll like my new rocking chair.

B. But I liked your OLD rocking chair. It was **comfortable**.

A. That's right. But my new rocking chair is **more comfortable**.

1. *apartment building*
   beautiful

2. *roommate*
   interesting

3. *girlfriend*
   intelligent

4. *boyfriend*
   handsome

5. *briefcase*
   attractive

6. *computer*
   powerful

7. *printer*
   fast

8. *English teacher*
   smart

9. *recipe for meatloaf*
   delicious

10. *boss*
    nice

11. *parrot*
    talkative

12.

Bicycles Are Safer Than Motorcycles

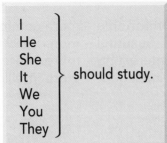

I
He
She
It
We
You
They

should study.

Should I study?

safe

useful

A. Should I buy a bicycle or a motorcycle?

B. I think you should buy a bicycle.

A. Why?

B. Bicycles are **safer than** motorcycles.

A. Should he study English or Latin?

B. I think he should study English.

A. Why?

B. English is **more useful than** Latin.

cheap

1. Should I buy a used car or a new car?

Ellen   Helen

interesting

2. Should he go out with Ellen or Helen?

friendly

3. Should she buy a dog or a cat?

honest

4. Should I vote for Linda Lee or Gary Green?

5. Should she take a course with Professor Blake or Professor Drake?

6. Should they plant flowers or vegetables this spring?

7. Should we buy this fan or that fan?

8. Should she buy these earrings or those earrings?

9. Should he take piano lessons with Mrs. Clark or Miss Smith?

10. Should I buy the hat in my left hand or the hat in my right hand?

11. Should she buy fur gloves or leather gloves?

12. Should I buy a notebook computer or a desktop computer?

13. Should I hire Ms. Parker or Ms. Jones?

14. Should I fire Mr. Mason or Mr. Grimes?

15. Should we rent this movie or that movie?

16.

READING

IT ISN'T EASY BEING A TEENAGER

I try to be a good son, but no matter how hard I try, my parents never seem to be satisfied. They think I should be a better* son. They think I should eat healthier food, I should wear nicer clothes, and I should get better grades. And according to them, my hair should be shorter, my room should be neater, and my friends should be more polite when they come to visit.

You know . . . it isn't easy being a teenager.

IT ISN'T EASY BEING PARENTS

We try to be good parents, but no matter how hard we try, our children never seem to be satisfied. They think we should be better parents. They think we should wear more fashionable clothes, we should drive a newer car, and we should listen to more interesting music. And according to them, we should be more sympathetic when they talk about their problems, we should be friendlier when their friends come to visit, and we should be more understanding when they come home late on Saturday night.

You know . . . it isn't easy being parents.

* good – better

✔ READING *CHECK-UP*

WHAT'S THE WORD?

According to this boy's parents, he doesn't eat __healthy__¹ food, he doesn't wear _____² clothes, he doesn't get _____³ grades, his hair isn't _____⁴, and his friends aren't _____⁵ when they come to visit.

According to their children, these parents don't wear _____⁶ clothes, they don't have a _____⁷ car, they don't listen to _____⁸ music, and they aren't _____⁹ when their children's friends come to visit.

LISTENING

Listen and choose what the people are talking about.

1. a. TV   b. printer
2. a. chair   b. recipe
3. a. hair   b. apartment

4. a. offices   b. friends
5. a. neighborhood   b. briefcase
6. a. rug   b. computer

Don't Be Ridiculous!

my – mine	our – ours
his – his	your – yours
her – hers	their – theirs

A. You know, my dog isn't as friendly as your dog.

B. Don't be ridiculous! Yours is MUCH friendlier than **mine**.

A. You know, my novels aren't as interesting as Ernest Hemingway's novels.

B. Don't be ridiculous! Yours are MUCH more interesting than **his**.

clean

powerful

nice

1. *my apartment*
   your apartment

2. *my computer*
   Bob's computer

3. *my boss*
   your boss

comfortable

big

She sells sea shells...
good

4. *my furniture*
   your furniture

5. *my house*
   the Jacksons' house

6. *my pronunciation*
   Maria's pronunciation

pretty

FRUITCAKE
delicious

7. *my garden*
   your garden

8. *my recipe for fruitcake*
   Stanley's recipe for fruitcake

9.

45

BROWNSVILLE

The Taylor family lived in Brownsville for many years. And for many years, Brownsville was a very good place to live. The streets were clean, the parks were safe, the bus system was reliable, and the schools were good.

But Brownsville changed. Today the streets aren't as clean as they used to be. The parks aren't as safe as they used to be. The bus system isn't as reliable as it used to be. And the schools aren't as good as they used to be.

Because of the changes in Brownsville, the Taylor family moved to Newport last year. In Newport the streets are cleaner, the parks are safer, the bus system is more reliable, and the schools are better. The Taylors are happy in Newport, but they were happier in Brownsville. Although Newport has cleaner streets, safer parks, a more reliable bus system, and better schools, Brownsville has friendlier people. They're nicer, more polite, and more hospitable than the people in Newport.

The Taylors miss Brownsville. Even though they're now living in Newport, Brownsville will always be their real home.

 READING CHECK-UP

Q & A

The people of Brownsville are calling Mayor Brown's radio talk show. They're upset about Brownsville's streets, parks, bus system, and schools. Using this model and the story, call Mayor Brown.

A. This is Mayor Brown. You're on the air.
B. Mayor Brown, I'm very upset about the *streets* here in Brownsville.
A. Why do you say that?
B. *They aren't* as *clean* as *they* used to be.
A. Do you really think so?
B. Definitely! You know . . . they say the *streets* in Newport *are cleaner*.
A. I'll see what I can do. Thank you for calling.

Agreeing & Disagreeing

A. { I think . . .
{ In my opinion, . . .

B. { I agree.
{ I agree with you.
{ I think so, too.

C. { I disagree.
{ I disagree with you.
{ I don't think so.

Practice interactions on this page, using these expressions for agreeing and disagreeing.

INTERACTIONS

_____er
}than
more _____

as _____ as
not as _____ as

I think New York is more interesting than Los Angeles.

I disagree. I think Los Angeles is MUCH more interesting than New York.

In my opinion, the weather in Honolulu is better than the weather in Miami.

I don't think so. I think the weather in Miami is better than the weather in Honolulu.

In my opinion, the people in Centerville aren't as friendly as the people in Greenville.

I agree. But the people in Centerville are more interesting.

I think so, too.

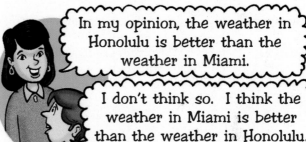

Practice conversations with other students. Compare different places you know.
Talk about . . .

the streets (_quiet, safe, clean, wide, busy_)
the buildings (_tall, modern, attractive_)
the weather (_cold, cool, warm, hot, rainy, snowy_)
the people (_friendly, nice, polite, honest, happy, hospitable, talkative, healthy_)
the city in general (_large, interesting, exciting, expensive_)

PRONUNCIATION Yes/No Questions with *or*

Listen. Then say it.

Should I buy a bicycle or a motorcycle?

Should we buy this fan or that fan?

Should he go out with Ellen or Helen?

Should she buy fur gloves or leather gloves?

Say it. Then listen.

Should they plant flowers or vegetables?

Should she buy these earrings or those earrings?

Should I hire Ms. Carter or Mr. Price?

Should I buy a notebook computer or a desktop computer?

SIDE by SIDE JOURNAL

In your journal, compare your home town and the place you live now. Or compare any two places you know.

GRAMMAR FOCUS

COMPARATIVES

My new car is	faster larger bigger prettier	than my old car.
	more comfortable more attractive	

SHOULD

Should	I he she it we you they	study?

I He She It We You They	should study.

POSSESSIVE PRONOUNS

This dog is nicer than	mine. his. hers. ours. yours. theirs.

Complete the sentences.

1. A. Is your new computer fast?
   B. Yes. It's _____ than my old computer.

2. A. Is Jane's new neighborhood safe?
   B. Yes. It's _____ than her old neighborhood.

3. A. Is Livingston an interesting city?
   B. Yes. I think it's _____ than Centerville.

4. A. Is your new office big?
   B. Yes. It's _____ than my old office.

5. A. Is your new sofa comfortable?
   B. Yes. It's _____ than our old sofa.

6. A. Should my grandparents get a dog or a cat?
   B. They _____ get a dog. Dogs are very friendly. I think they're _____ than cats.

7. A. Should I order the chicken or the fish?
   B. I think you _____ order the fish. It's really good. It's _____ than the chicken.

Match the sentences.

____ 1. Is this your hat or your son's hat?

____ 2. Is this your pen or your wife's pen?

____ 3. Is this my jacket or your jacket?

____ 4. Is this your cat or your neighbors' cat?

____ 5. Is this Lucy's key or her brother's key?

a. It isn't yours. It's mine.

b. It isn't hers. It's his.

c. It isn't mine. It's hers.

d. It isn't mine. It's his.

e. It isn't ours. It's theirs.

Superlatives

- **Describing People, Places, and Things**
- **Shopping in a Department Store**
- **Expressing Opinions**

VOCABULARY PREVIEW

1. energetic	6. lazy	11. patient
2. funny	7. mean	12. popular
3. generous	8. nice	13. rude
4. helpful	9. noisy	14. sloppy
5. honest	10. obnoxious	15. stubborn

49

The Smartest Person I Know

smart – the smartest kind – the kindest	nice – the nicest safe – the safest
funny – the funniest pretty – the prettiest	big – the biggest hot – the hottest

A. I think your friend Margaret is very **smart**.

B. She certainly is. She's **the smartest** person I know.

1. *your Aunt Emma*
   kind

2. *your friend Jim*
   bright

3. *your parents*
   nice

4. *your Uncle Ted*
   funny

5. *your sister*
   pretty

6. *your cousin Amy*
   friendly

7. *Larry*
   lazy

8. *your landlord*
   mean

9. *your roommates*
   sloppy

The Most Energetic Person I Know

smart – the smartest
funny – the funniest
nice – the nicest
big – the biggest

energetic – the most energetic
interesting – the most interesting
patient – the most patient
stubborn – the most stubborn

A. I think your grandmother is very **energetic**.

B. She certainly is. She's **the most energetic** person I know.

1. *your friend Carlos interesting*

2. *your grandfather generous*

3. *your cousins talented*

4. *our English teacher patient*

5. *your nephew Andrew stubborn*

6. *your younger brother polite*

7. *your older sister bright*

8. *your upstairs neighbor noisy*

9. *your downstairs neighbor rude*

10. *Senator Smith honest*

11. *our history professor boring*

12.

THE NICEST PERSON

friendly | polite | smart | talented | pretty

Mr. and Mrs. Jackson are very proud of their daughter, Linda. She's a very nice person. She's friendly, she's polite, she's smart, and she's talented. She's also very pretty.

Mr. and Mrs. Jackson's friends and neighbors always compliment them about Linda. They say she's the nicest person they know. According to them, she's the friendliest, the most polite, the smartest, and the most talented girl in the neighborhood. They also think she's the prettiest.

Mr. and Mrs. Jackson agree. They think Linda is a wonderful girl, and they're proud to say she's their daughter.

THE MOST OBNOXIOUS DOG

noisy | stubborn | lazy | mean | ugly

Mr. and Mrs. Hubbard are very embarrassed by their dog, Rex. He's a very obnoxious dog. He's noisy, he's stubborn, he's lazy, and he's mean. He's also very ugly.

Mr. and Mrs. Hubbard's friends and neighbors always complain about Rex. They say he's the most obnoxious dog they know. According to them, he's the noisiest, the most stubborn, the laziest, and the meanest dog in the neighborhood. They also think he's the ugliest.

Mr. and Mrs. Hubbard agree. They think Rex is a horrible dog, and they're ashamed to say he's theirs.

✓ READING CHECK-UP

CHOOSE

1. Linda is the (most polite   smart) person I know.
2. She's the most (talented   friendliest) girl in the neighborhood.
3. She's a very (nicest   nice) person.
4. Rex is the most (stubborn   mean) dog in the neighborhood.
5. He's the (lazy   noisiest) dog I know.
6. He's also the most (ugliest   obnoxious) dog in town.

Q & A

The neighbors are talking. Using these models, create dialogs based on the stories.

A. You know . . . I think Linda is very *nice*.
B. I agree. She's the *nicest* girl in the neighborhood.

A. You know . . . I think Rex is very *obnoxious*.
B. You're right. He's the *most obnoxious* dog in the neighborhood.

How About You?

Tell about the nicest person you know.

How to Say It!

Expressing an Opinion

A. { In my opinion, . . .
    As far as I'm concerned, . . .
    If you ask me, . . . } *Linda is the most talented student in our school.*

B. I agree. / I disagree.

Practice conversations with other students. Share opinions.

LISTENING

Listen to the sentence. Is the person saying something good or something bad about someone else?

1. a. good   b. bad
2. a. good   b. bad
3. a. good   b. bad
4. a. good   b. bad
5. a. good   b. bad
6. a. good   b. bad
7. a. good   b. bad
8. a. good   b. bad
9. a. good   b. bad

PRONUNCIATION *Linking Words with Duplicated Consonants*

Listen. Then say it.

She's the nicest teacher in our school.

He's the most stubborn neighbor on our street.

They're the most talented dancers in the world.

Say it. Then listen.

He's the most generous student in our class.

This is the cheapest toothpaste in the store.

He's the most polite taxi driver in the city.

I Want to Buy a Small Radio

a small radio
a smaller radio
the smallest radio

a comfortable chair
a more comfortable chair
the most comfortable chair

a good car
a better car
the best car

A. May I help you?

B. Yes, please. I want to buy a **small** radio.

A. I think you'll like this one. It's VERY **small**.

B. Don't you have a **smaller** one?

A. No, I'm afraid not. This is **the smallest** one we have.

B. Thank you anyway.

A. Sorry we can't help you. Please come again.

A. May I help you?

B. Yes, please. I want to buy a/an _____ _____.

A. I think you'll like this one. It's VERY _____.

B. Don't you have a/an { _____er / more _____ } one?

A. No, I'm afraid not. This is the { _____est / most _____ } one we have.

B. Thank you anyway.

A. Sorry we can't help you. Please come again.

1. *large TV*

2. *comfortable rocking chair*

3. *good CD player*

4. *cheap watch*

5. *fast printer*

6. *elegant evening gown*

7. *small cell phone*

8. *lightweight video camera*

9. *powerful computer*

10. *tall bookcase*

11. *short novel*

12.

BOB'S BARGAIN DEPARTMENT STORE

Bob's Bargain Department Store is the cheapest store in town. However, even though it's the cheapest, it isn't the most popular. People don't shop there very often because the products are bad.* In fact, some people say the products there are the worst in town.

The furniture isn't very comfortable, the clothes aren't very fashionable, the appliances aren't very dependable, and the home entertainment products aren't very good. Besides that, the location isn't very convenient, and the salespeople aren't very helpful.

That's why people don't shop at Bob's Bargain Department Store very often, even though it's the cheapest store in town.

THE LORD AND LADY DEPARTMENT STORE

The Lord and Lady Department Store sells very good products. In fact, some people say the products there are the best in town.

They sell the most comfortable furniture, the most fashionable clothes, the most dependable appliances, and the best home entertainment products. And besides that, their location is the most convenient, and their salespeople are the most helpful in town.

However, even though the Lord and Lady Department Store is the best store in town, people don't shop there very often because it's also the most expensive.

* bad – worse – worst

THE SUPER SAVER DEPARTMENT STORE

The Super Saver Department Store is the most popular store in town. It isn't the cheapest, and it isn't the most expensive. It doesn't have the best products, and it doesn't have the worst.

The furniture isn't the most comfortable you can buy, but it's more comfortable than the furniture at many other stores. The clothes aren't the most fashionable you can buy, but they're more fashionable than the clothes at many other stores. The appliances aren't the most dependable you can buy, but they're more dependable than the appliances at many other stores. The home entertainment products aren't the best you can buy, but they're better than the home entertainment products at many other stores. In addition, the location is convenient, and the salespeople are helpful.

You can see why the Super Saver Department Store is the most popular store in town. The prices are reasonable, and the products are good. That's why people like to shop there.

 READING *CHECK-UP*

TRUE OR FALSE?

1. Bob's Bargain Department Store is the most popular store in town.
2. The salespeople at Lord and Lady are more helpful than the salespeople at Super Saver.
3. The location of Lord and Lady isn't as convenient as the location of Bob's.
4. The Super Saver Department Store has the best prices in town.
5. The home entertainment products at Super Saver are better than the home entertainment products at Bob's.
6. People in this town say the cheapest department store is the best.

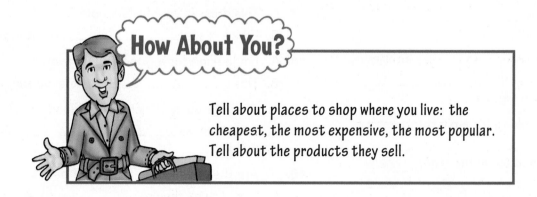

How About You?

Tell about places to shop where you live: the cheapest, the most expensive, the most popular. Tell about the products they sell.

INTERACTIONS *Sharing Opinions*

Practice conversations with other students. Share opinions, and give reasons for your opinions.

In your opinion, . . .

1. Who is the most popular actor/actress in your country? Who is the most popular TV star? the best singer?

2. What is the most popular car in your country? the most popular sport? the best newspaper? the most popular magazine? the best TV program? the most popular food?

3. What is the best city in your country? What is the worst city? Why? What are the most interesting tourist sights in your country? What are the most popular vacation places?

4. Who is the most important person in your country now? Why? Who was the most important person in the history of your country? Why?

SIDE by SIDE JOURNAL

Who is the most important person in your life? Why? Write about this person in your journal.

GRAMMAR FOCUS

SUPERLATIVES

| He's | the smartest the nicest the biggest the busiest | person I know. |
| | the most talented the most interesting | |

Complete the sentences.

1. A. I'm looking for a fast computer.
   B. This is _____ computer we sell.

2. A. Your sister Susan is very intelligent.
   B. I agree. She's _____ person I know.

3. A. I'm looking for a big refrigerator.
   B. This is _____ refrigerator in the store.

4. A. Our cousins are very nice.
   B. I agree. They're _____ people in our family.

5. A. Is this camera lightweight?
   B. Yes. It's _____ camera you can find.

6. A. Our history teacher is very interesting.
   B. I agree. I think he's _____ teacher in the school.

7. A. This dress is very fashionable.
   B. I think it's _____ dress in the store.

8. A. I'm looking for a good DVD player.
   B. This is _____ one we sell.

9. A. Are your upstairs neighbors friendly?
   B. Yes. They're _____ people in our building.

10. A. Are the products at that store bad?
    B. Yes. I think they're _____ products in town.

Did You Know?

The longest car in the world is 100 feet long. It has 26 wheels, a swimming pool, and a waterbed!

The world's biggest costume party is the Carnival celebration in Brazil. Every day during Carnival, more than 50,000 people walk through the streets in costumes.

The largest subway station in the world is Grand Central Terminal in New York City. Every day more than half a million people pass through the station.

The biggest igloo in the world is the Ice Hotel in Sweden. It has rooms for 150 guests. Every year workers have to rebuild the hotel because it melts in the spring!

FACT FILE

World Geography Facts

- The longest river in the world is the Nile. It is 4,180 miles (6,690 kilometers) long.

- The largest ocean in the world is the Pacific Ocean. It is 64,000,000 square miles (165,760,000 square kilometers).

- The highest mountain in the world is Mount Everest. It is 29,028 feet (8,848 meters) high.

- The biggest desert in the world is the Sahara. It is 3,500,270 square miles (9,065,000 square kilometers).

BUILD YOUR VOCABULARY!

Adjectives with Negative Prefixes

They're _____ .

 ■ uncomfortable

 ■ unfriendly

 ■ unhealthy

 ■ unsafe

 ■ impatient

 ■ impolite

 ■ inexpensive

 ■ dishonest

AROUND THE WORLD

Recreation and Entertainment

The most popular type of outdoor recreation in France is camping. Every night 3 million people in France sleep outside.

Movies are the most popular type of entertainment in India. Every day 15 million people in India go to the movies.

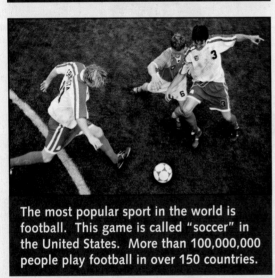

The most popular sport in the world is football. This game is called "soccer" in the United States. More than 100,000,000 people play football in over 150 countries.

What are the most popular types of recreation and entertainment in different countries you know?

Global Exchange

IvanaG: I'm going on vacation with my family tomorrow. We're going to the most popular beach in our country. We'll stay there for a week in a small hotel. It isn't the best hotel there, but it's the friendliest and the closest to the beach. We go there every year. It's a lot of fun! The water is clear, and the air is fresh. My sister and my brother and I swim all day, and we go to an amusement park in the evening. I think it has the largest roller-coaster in the world! So I'll write again when I get back and tell you all about our vacation.

P.S. Do you have a favorite vacation place? Where is it? When do you go there? What do you do?

Send a message to a keypal. Tell about a favorite vacation place in your country.

LISTENING

And Now a Word From Our Sponsors!

_b_ **1** Rings & Things   **a.** furniture

____ **2** Big Value Store   **b.** jewelry

____ **3** Comfort Kingdom   **c.** sports equipment

____ **4** Electric City   **d.** appliances

____ **5** Recreation Station   **e.** home entertainment products

---

What Are They Saying?

The biggest !
The smallest !
The fastest !
The most exciting !

Imperatives
Directions

- **Getting Around Town**   • **Public Transportation**

VOCABULARY PREVIEW

1. airport	6. hardware store	11. pet shop
2. baseball stadium	7. ice cream shop	12. playground
3. concert hall	8. motel	13. shoe store
4. courthouse	9. museum	14. toy store
5. flower shop	10. parking garage	15. university

Can You Tell Me How to Get to . . . ?

walk up
walk down

on the right
on the left

across from
next to
between

MAIN ST.

drug store	laundromat
barber shop	bakery
toy store	clinic
bank	shoe store
police station	high school
library	post office

laundromat?

A. Excuse me. Can you tell me how to get to the laundromat from here?

B. Sure. **Walk up** Main Street and you'll see the laundromat **on the right, across from** the drug store.

A. Thank you.

post office?

A. Excuse me. Can you tell me how to get to the post office from here?

B. Sure. **Walk down** Main Street and you'll see the post office **on the left, next to** the high school.

A. Thank you.

1. *clinic?*

2. *police station?*

3. *drug store?*

4. *library?*

5. *barber shop?*

6. *toy store?*

62

Could You Please Tell Me How to Get to . . . ?

walk along	on the right on the left	across from next to between

A. Excuse me. Could you please tell me how to get to the hospital from here?

B. Sure. **Walk along** Central Avenue and you'll see the hospital **on the left, between** the museum and the park.

A. Thanks.

hospital?

1. *museum?*

2. *university?*

3. *park?*

4. *hotel?*

5. *parking lot?*

6. *zoo?*

Would You Please Tell Me How to Get to . . . ?

turn left   turn right

bus station?

A. Excuse me. Would you please tell me how to get to the bus station from here?

B. Certainly. **Walk up** Park Street to Second Avenue and **turn right**. **Walk along** Second Avenue and you'll see the bus station **on the left, across from** the cafeteria.

A. Thanks very much.

concert hall?

A. Excuse me. Would you please tell me how to get to the concert hall from here?

B. Certainly. **Drive along** Second Avenue to River Street and **turn left**. **Drive up** River Street and you'll see the concert hall **on the right, between** the courthouse and the church.

A. Thanks very much.

1. *hospital?*

2. *zoo?*

3. *shoe store?*

4. *laundromat?*

5. *supermarket?*

6. *post office?*

7. *clinic?*

8. *airport?*

9.

How to Say It!

Asking for Repetition

A. I'm sorry. Could you please { repeat that?
say that again?

B. Sure. *Walk along . . .*

**Practice some conversations on this page again.
Ask people to repeat the directions.**

Take the Main Street Bus

A. Excuse me. What's the quickest way to get to Peter's Pet Shop?

B. **Take** the Main Street bus and **get off** at First Avenue. **Walk up** First Avenue and you'll see Peter's Pet Shop **on the right**.

A. Thank you very much.

B. You're welcome.

A. Excuse me. What's the easiest way to get to Harry's Barber Shop?

B. **Take** the subway and **get off** at Fourth Avenue. **Walk down** Fourth Avenue and you'll see Harry's Barber Shop **on the left**.

A. Thank you very much.

B. You're welcome.

1. What's the fastest way to get to the baseball stadium?

2. What's the best way to get to the library?

3. What's the most direct way to get to the zoo?

4. I'm in a hurry! What's the shortest way to get to the train station?

ROLE PLAY *Can You Tell Me How to Get There?*

A. Can you recommend **a good hotel**?

B. Yes. The Bellview is **a good hotel**. I think it's **one of the best hotels** in town.

A. Can you tell me how to get there?

B. Sure. Take the subway and get off at Brighton Boulevard. You'll see the Bellview at the corner of Brighton Boulevard and Twelfth Street.

A. Thank you very much.

B. You're welcome.

These people are visiting your city. Recommend real places you know and like, and give directions.

Can you recommend a good restaurant?

Can you recommend a big department store?

Can you recommend an interesting tourist sight?

Can you recommend _____?

HAROLD NEVER GOT THERE!

Dear Students,

Here are directions to my house. I'll see you at the party.

Your English teacher

1. From our school, walk along Main St. to Central Ave. and turn left.

2. Walk up Central Ave. 2 blocks, and you'll see a bus stop at the corner, across from the post office.

3. Take the Central Ave. bus and get off at Fifth St.

4. Turn left and walk along Fifth St. 3 blocks to Park Ave. and turn right.

5. Walk up Park Ave. 1 block, and you'll see a bus stop at the corner of Park Ave. and Sixth St.

6. Take Bus #42 and get off at Rolling Rd.

7. Turn left and walk along Rolling Rd. 1 block.

8. Turn left again, and walk 2 blocks to Holly Lane and turn right.

9. Walk along Holly Lane. My house is the last one on the right.

Harold was very disappointed last night. All the other students in his English class went to a party at their teacher's house, but Harold never got there. He followed his teacher's directions, but he made one little mistake.

From their school, he walked along Main Street to Central Avenue and turned left. He walked up Central Avenue two blocks to the bus stop at the corner, across from the post office. He took the Central Avenue bus and got off at Fifth Street. He turned left and walked along Fifth Street three blocks to Park Avenue and turned right. He walked up Park Avenue one block to the bus stop at the corner of Park Avenue and Sixth Street.

He took Bus Number 42, but he got off at the wrong stop. He got off at River Road instead of Rolling Road. He turned left and walked along River Road one block. He turned left again and walked two blocks, turned right, and got completely lost.

Harold was very upset. He really wanted to go to the party last night, and he can't believe he made such a stupid mistake!

✔ READING CHECK-UP

TRUE OR FALSE?

1. Harold's English teacher lives on Holly Lane.
2. The Central Avenue bus stops across from the post office.
3. The teacher made one little mistake in the directions.
4. The school is on Main Street.
5. Harold took the wrong bus.
6. Bus Number 42 goes to Rolling Road.
7. Harold got off the bus at Rolling Road.
8. Harold didn't really want to go to the party last night.

WHAT'S THE WORD?

It's very easy to get _____1 the zoo from here. Walk up this street _____2 the corner and turn right. Walk two blocks and you'll see a bus stop _____3 the corner _____4 Grove Street and Fourth Avenue. Take the West Side bus and get _____5 _____6 Park Road. You'll see the zoo _____7 the left. It's next _____8 the library and across _____9 the museum.

LISTENING

WHAT'S THE WORD?

Listen and choose the word you hear.

1. a. right   b. left
2. a. right   b. left
3. a. down   b. up
4. a. along   b. down
5. a. to   b. on
6. a. off   b. of
7. a. on   b. at

WHERE ARE THEY?

Where are these people? Listen and choose the correct place.

1. a. department store   b. laundromat
2. a. pet shop   b. cafeteria
3. a. restaurant   b. library
4. a. hospital   b. hotel
5. a. barber shop   b. supermarket
6. a. parking lot   b. parking garage

IN YOUR OWN WORDS

FOR WRITING AND DISCUSSION

You're going to invite people to your home. Draw a map and write directions to help them get there. (Give them directions from your school.)

PRONUNCIATION   *Could you & Would you*

Listen. Then say it.

Could you please tell me how to get to the bank?

Could you please repeat that?

Would you please tell me how to get to the library?

Say it. Then listen.

Could you please tell me how to get to the park?

Could you please say that again?

Would you please tell me how to get to the zoo?

How do you get to different places in your community? Do you walk? Do you drive? Do you take a bus, train, or subway? Is it easy or difficult to get to these places? Write about it in your journal.

GRAMMAR FOCUS

IMPERATIVES

Walk up Main Street.	**Turn right.**	**Take** the Main Street bus.
Walk down Main Street.	**Turn left.**	**Get off** at First Avenue.
Walk along Central Avenue.		**Drive along** Second Avenue.

Choose the correct word.

1. Turn (along   **left**).
2. (Take   Walk) the River Street bus.
3. Get (up   off) at Central Avenue.
4. Walk (up   right) Third Avenue.
5. (Drive   Turn) along Park Street.
6. (Walk   Get) off the bus at Fourth Avenue.

Complete these directions with the following words.

across	at	corner	on	Take	turn	Walk
and	blocks	get	see	to	two	

It's easy to get to the hospital from here. Walk up this street _____[1] the corner and _____[2] right. _____[3] three _____[4] and you'll _____[5] a bus stop at the _____[6] of Park Street _____[7] Tenth Avenue. _____[8] the Park Street bus and _____[9] off _____[10] University Road. Walk _____[11] blocks and you'll see the hospital _____[12] the right, _____[13] from the bus station.

ACTIVITY WORKBOOK

SIDE by SIDE Extra

2A

Steven J. Molinsky
Bill Bliss

with
Carolyn Graham • Peter S. Bliss

Contributing Authors
Dorothy Lynde • Elizabeth Handley

Illustrated by
Richard E. Hill

CONTENTS

A WHAT DO THEY LIKE TO DO?

chat online	go hiking	go to the mall	play soccer	write letters
go dancing	go to the beach	listen to music	watch TV	

STUDENT BOOK
PAGES **1–10**

1. He _____ *likes to* _____

_____ *watch TV* _____.

2. They _____.

3. She _____

_____.

4. I _____

_____.

5. They _____

_____.

6. He _____

_____.

7. She _____

_____.

8. We _____

_____.

9. My dog _____

_____.

B LISTENING

Listen and choose the correct response.

1. a. He likes to chat online.
    b. They like to chat online.

2. a. I like to dance.
    b. She likes to dance.

3. a. He likes to read.
    b. She likes to read.

4. a. They like to play basketball.
    b. We like to play basketball.

5. a. He likes to go to the library.
    b. We like to go to the library.

6. a. You like to go to the mall.
    b. I like to go to the mall.

7. a. We like to play loud music.
    b. He likes to play loud music.

8. a. She likes to watch TV.
    b. They like to watch TV.

2   Activity Workbook

C WHAT DO THEY LIKE TO DO?

bake	go	listen	ride	sing	watch

1. Alan likes to _____watch_____ TV.

   _____He watches_____ TV every day.

   _____He watched_____ TV yesterday.

   _____He's going to watch_____ TV tomorrow.

2. I like to _____ to music.

   _____ to music every day.

   _____ to music yesterday.

   _____ to music tomorrow.

3. Thelma likes to _____ her bicycle.

   _____ her bicycle every day.

   _____ her bicycle yesterday.

   _____ her bicycle tomorrow.

4. My parents like to _____.

   _____ every day.

   _____ yesterday.

   _____ tomorrow.

5. My wife and I like to _____ cookies.

   _____ cookies every day.

   _____ cookies yesterday.

   _____ cookies tomorrow.

6. Brian likes to _____ sailing.

   _____ sailing every day.

   _____ sailing yesterday.

   _____ sailing tomorrow.

Activity Workbook   **3**

D LIKES AND DISLIKES

clean	cook	drive	eat	feed	go	read	take	wait	watch

<table>
<tr><td>like to
likes to</td><td>don't like to
doesn't like to</td></tr>
</table>

1. Ronald _____likes to cook_____ spaghetti.

2. Sally ___doesn't like to take___ the subway.

3. My children _____ the birds in the park.

4. Ted and Amy _____ in noisy restaurants.

5. My wife _____ novels.

6. Arnold _____ for the bus.

7. My friends and I _____ videos.

8. I _____ downtown.

9. Howard _____ his house.

10. Tim and Jim _____ to the doctor.

WRITE ABOUT YOURSELF

What do you like to do?

I like to ....

I ....

I ....

I ....

I ....

What don't you like to do?

I don't like to ....

I ....

I ....

I ....

I ....

F **DAY AFTER DAY**

| do | get up | go | make | plant | play | study | visit | wash | write |

1. Tim _____*washes*_____ his car every day.

   _____*He washed*_____ his car yesterday.

   _____*He's going to wash*_____ his car tomorrow.

2. Alice _____ early every morning.

   _____ early yesterday morning.

   _____ early tomorrow morning.

3. Millie and Max _____ dancing every Friday.

   _____ dancing last Friday.

   _____ dancing next Friday.

4. I _____ English every evening.

   _____ English yesterday evening.

   _____ English tomorrow evening.

(continued)

5. The man next door _____ the drums every night.

_____ the drums last night.

_____ the drums tomorrow night.

6. My mother _____ pancakes for breakfast every Sunday.

_____ pancakes last Sunday.

_____ pancakes next Sunday.

7. My wife and I _____ flowers every spring.

_____ flowers last spring.

_____ flowers next spring.

8. Steven _____ to his girlfriend every week.

_____ to her last week.

_____ to her next week.

9. Julie _____ her grandparents every weekend.

_____ them last weekend.

_____ them next weekend.

10. My husband and I _____ yoga every afternoon.

_____ yoga yesterday afternoon.

_____ yoga tomorrow afternoon.

11. I .... every ....

....

....

GRAMMARRAP: *I Don't Like to Rush*

Listen. Then clap and practice.

I	don't like to	rush.	Do you?
I	don't like to	hurry.	
I	don't like to	get	upset.
I	don't like to	worry.	

I'm not	going to	rush.	Are you?
I'm not	going to	hurry.	
I'm not	going to	get	upset.
I'm not	going to	worry!	

H **GRAMMARRAP:** *He Doesn't Like to Watch TV*

Listen. Then clap and practice.

He doesn't	like to	watch	TV.
He doesn't	like to	dance.	
He doesn't	like to	cook or	sew
or wash or	iron his	pants.	

She doesn't	like to	go to the	beach.
She doesn't	like to	shop.	
She doesn't	like to	vacuum her	rugs
or dust or	wax or	mop.	

I WHAT'S PAULA GOING TO GIVE HER FAMILY?

cell phone
gloves
CD player
novel
dog
plant
watch
sweater

Paula is looking for presents for her family. Here's what she's going to give them.

1. Her husband's hands are always cold.   _____She's going to give him gloves._____

2. Her daughter loves animals.   _____

3. Her son never arrives on time.   _____

4. Her parents like to listen to music.   _____

5. Her sister likes clothes.   _____

6. Her brother likes to read.   _____

7. Her grandparents like flowers.   _____

8. Her cousin Charlie likes to talk to his friends.   _____

J PRESENTS

1. Last year I ____gave____ my husband pajamas.   This year _____I'm going to give him_____ a bathrobe.

2. Last year Bobby _____ his grandmother candy.   This year _____ flowers.

3. Last year Carol _____ her boyfriend a tee shirt.   This year _____ sweat pants.

4. Last year we _____ our children a bird.   This year _____ a dog.

5. Last year I _____ my girlfriend perfume.   This year _____ a ring.

6. Last year we _____ our son a sweater.   This year _____ a bicycle.

7. Last year I ....   This year ....

| he | her | him | I | me | she | they | them | us | we | you |

1. A. What did you give your wife for her birthday?

   B. _____I_____ gave _____her_____ earrings.

2. A. What did your children give you for your birthday?

   B. _____ gave _____ a book.

3. A. What did Michael give his parents for their anniversary?

   B. _____ gave _____ a CD player.

4. A. What did your friends give you and your husband for your anniversary?

   B. _____ gave _____ a plant.

5. A. What did your wife give you for your birthday?

   B. _____ gave _____ a briefcase.

6. A. What did you and your wife give your son for his birthday?

   B. _____ gave _____ a bicycle.

7. A. I forget. What did you give me for my last birthday?

   B. _____ gave _____ a painting.

8. A. I forget. What did I give you for *your* last birthday?

   B. _____ gave _____ a dress.

Activity Workbook   **9**

1st	first	7th	seventh	13th	thirteenth	19th	nineteenth	50th	fiftieth
2nd	second	8th	eighth	14th	fourteenth	20th	twentieth	60th	sixtieth
3rd	third	9th	ninth	15th	fifteenth	21st	twenty-first	70th	seventieth
4th	fourth	10th	tenth	16th	sixteenth	22nd	twenty-second	80th	eightieth
5th	fifth	11th	eleventh	17th	seventeenth	30th	thirtieth	90th	ninetieth
6th	sixth	12th	twelfth	18th	eighteenth	40th	fortieth	100th	one hundredth

L MATCHING

_b_ 1. eighth   a. 2nd   ____ 5. thirty-third   e. 14th

____ 2. one hundredth   b. 8th   ____ 6. thirteenth   f. 13th

____ 3. second   c. 20th   ____ 7. fourteenth   g. 40th

____ 4. twentieth   d. 100th   ____ 8. fortieth   h. 33rd

M WHAT'S THE NUMBER?

1. fiftieth   ___50th___   6. first   _____

2. ninety-ninth   _____   7. sixteenth   _____

3. fifteenth   _____   8. sixty-fifth   _____

4. twelfth   _____   9. eighty-fourth _____

5. seventy-seventh   _____   10. thirty-sixth   _____

N LISTENING

Listen and write the ordinal number you hear.

1. barber shop   ___2nd___

2. Wong family   _____

3. Acme Company   _____

4. Bob Richards   _____

5. bank   _____

6. dentist's office   _____

7. flower shop   _____

8. Martinez family   _____

9. Louise Lane   _____

10. computer store   _____

11. French restaurant _____

12. my apartment   _____

13. Park family   _____

14. Dr. Jacobson   _____

15. Walker family   _____

16. health club   _____

O RICHARD'S BIRTHDAYS

Fill in the missing words.

On Richard's 7th birthday, he (have) ___had___¹ a party at home. His mother (make) _____² pizza, and his father (bake) _____³ a cake. Richard's parents (give) _____⁴ him a new dog. Richard's friends (love) _____⁵ his birthday party because they (play) _____⁶ with his new dog, but Richard was upset because his mother didn't (give) _____⁷ the dog any cake to eat.

On Richard's 10th birthday, he (go) _____⁸ to the beach with his friends. They (swim) _____⁹ at the beach, and they (go) _____¹⁰ to a restaurant to eat. Richard's friends (like) _____¹¹ his birthday party, but Richard was upset because he didn't (like) _____¹² his present. His friends (give) _____¹³ him a wallet, but he (want) _____¹⁴ a baseball.

On Richard's 13th birthday, he (have) _____¹⁵ a picnic. His mother (cook) _____¹⁶ hot dogs and hamburgers. They (eat) _____¹⁷ delicious food and (play) _____¹⁸ baseball. All of his friends (enjoy) _____¹⁹ his birthday party, but Richard was upset because the girls didn't (talk) _____²⁰ to him.

On Richard's 16th birthday, he didn't (have) _____²¹ a party. He (go) _____²² dancing with his girlfriend, and he (have) _____²³ a wonderful time. His friends didn't (give) _____²⁴ him presents and his parents didn't (cook) _____²⁵. But Richard wasn't upset because he (dance) _____²⁶ with his girlfriend all night.

P MATCHING

_b_	**1.** Richard didn't like his present _____.	**a.**	on his 7th birthday
____	**2.** He went dancing _____.	**b.**	on his 10th birthday
____	**3.** His parents gave him a dog _____.	**c.**	on his 13th birthday
____	**4.** The girls didn't talk to Richard _____.	**d.**	on his 16th birthday

Activity Workbook   11

A WHAT'S THE FOOD?

apples	cheese	ice cream	meat	pepper
bread	eggs	ketchup	mustard	potatoes
cake	flour	lettuce	onions	soy sauce
carrots	grapes	mayonnaise	oranges	tomatoes

STUDENT BOOK
PAGES **11–18**

1. _____tomatoes_____   2. _____   3. _____   4. _____

5. _____   6. _____   7. _____   8. _____

9. _____   10. _____   11. _____   12. _____

13. _____   14. _____   15. _____   16. _____

17. _____   18. _____   19. _____   20. _____

12   Activity Workbook

WHAT ARE THEY SAYING?

Where's	Where are	It's	They're

1. A. ____Where's____ the butter?

   B. ____It's____ in the refrigerator.

2. A. ____Where are____ the bananas?

   B. ____They're____ on the counter.

3. A. _____ the salt?

   B. _____ in the cabinet.

4. A. _____ the lemons?

   B. _____ in the refrigerator.

5. A. _____ the cookies?

   B. _____ in the cabinet.

6. A. _____ the chicken?

   B. _____ in the freezer.

7. A. _____ the pears?

   B. _____ on the counter.

8. A. _____ the rice?

   B. _____ in the cabinet.

C **LISTENING**

Listen and choose the correct response.

1. a. It's on the counter.
   b. They're on the counter.

2. a. It's in the refrigerator.
   b. They're in the refrigerator.

3. a. It's in the freezer.
   b. They're in the freezer.

4. a. It's in the cabinet.
   b. They're in the cabinet.

5. a. It's on the counter.
   b. They're on the counter.

6. a. It's in the cabinet.
   b. They're in the cabinet.

7. a. It's on the counter.
   b. They're on the counter.

8. a. It's in the refrigerator.
   b. They're in the refrigerator.

Look at the menu to see what Randy's Restaurant has and doesn't have today.

Today's Menu
spaghetti
hamburgers
salad
ice cream
apple pie
milk
soda

1. A. May I have a hamburger and some french fries?

    B. I'm sorry, but _____ there aren't _____

    _____ any french fries _____ .

2. A. May I please have a salad and some tea?

    B. I'm sorry, but _____ there isn't _____

    _____ any tea _____ .

3. A. May I have chicken and some milk?

    B. I'm sorry, but _____

    _____ .

4. A. May I have ice cream and some cookies?

    B. I'm sorry, but _____

    _____ .

5. A. May I have cake and some soda?

    B. I'm sorry, but _____

    _____ .

6. A. May we have two sandwiches, please?

    B. I'm sorry, but _____

    _____ .

7. A. May I have apple pie and some orange juice?

    B. I'm sorry, but _____

    _____ .

8. A. May I have spaghetti and some meatballs?

    B. I'm sorry, but _____

    _____ .

1. There _____isn't any mayonnaise_____.

   How about some _____mustard_____?

2. There _____aren't any bananas_____.

   How about some _____grapes_____?

3. There _____.

   How about some _____?

4. There _____.

   How about some _____?

5. There _____.

   How about some _____?

6. There _____.

   How about some _____?

7. There _____.

   How about some _____?

8. There _____.

   How about some _____?

F LISTENING

Listen and put a check (✓) under the correct picture.

1. _____ ✔ 2. _____ _____ 3. _____ _____

4. _____ _____ 5. _____ _____ 6. _____ _____

G WHAT'S THE WORD?

how much	too much	how many	too many	a little	a few

1. A. _____How many_____ meatballs do you want?

   B. Not _____too many_____.

   Just _____a few_____.

2. A. _____How much_____ cheese do you want?

   B. Not _____too much_____.

   Just _____a little_____.

3. A. _____ ice cream do you want?

   B. Not _____.

   Just _____.

4. A. _____ cookies do you want?

   B. Not _____.

   Just _____.

5. A. _____ lemonade do you want?

   B. Not _____.

   Just _____.

6. A. _____ oranges do you want?

   B. Not _____.

   Just _____.

H WHAT'S THE PROBLEM?

too much	too many

1. She cooked _____too many_____ meatballs.

2. He drinks _____ soda.

3. They ate _____ ice cream.

4. Henry had _____ onions.

16 Activity Workbook

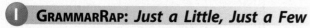
Listen. Then clap and practice.

A.   How much   salt should I   put in the   soup?

B.   Just   a little,   not too   much.

A.   How many   onions should I   put in the   salad?

B.   Just   a few,   not too   many.

A.   How much   pepper should I   put in the   stew?

B.   Just   a little,   not too   much.

A.   How many   eggs should I   put in the   omelet?

B.   Just   a few,   not too   many.

A.   How much   sugar should I   put in the   tea?

B.   Just   a little,   not too   much.

All.   Salt in the   soup,

       Pepper in the   stew,

       Eggs in the   omelet,

       Just   a few.

       Just   a little,   not too   much.

       Not too   many,   just   a few.

       Just   a few,   not too   many.

       Not too   many,   just one or   two.

little	much	this	is	it's	it
few	many	these	are	they're	them

1. A. Would you care for some more chocolate cake?

   B. Yes, please. But only a ___little___.

   My dentist says I eat too ___much___ chocolate cake.

2. A. Would you care for some more french fries?

   B. Yes, please. But only a _____.

   My wife says I eat too _____ french fries.

3. A. _____ pizza _____ fantastic.

   B. I'm glad you like _____. Would you

   care for a _____ more?

   A. Yes, please.

4. A. _____ potatoes _____ good.

   B. I'm glad you like _____. Would you

   care for a _____ more?

   A. No, thank you.

5. A. Would you like a _____ yogurt?

   B. Yes, please. My doctor says _____ good for my health.

6. A. Would you care for some cookies? I

   baked _____ this morning.

   B. Yes, please. But just a _____.

7. A. Would you care for some more pie?

   B. Yes, please. I know _____ bad for

   my health, but I really like _____.

8. A. You're eating too _____ meatballs!

   B. I know. But _____ really good.

   Can I have just a _____ more?

_e_   **1.** This pie is very good!

_____   **2.** How do you like the hamburgers?

_____   **3.** I think these cookies are excellent!

_____   **4.** How much rice do you want?

_____   **5.** Where's the tea?

_____   **6.** Let's make some lemonade!

_____   **7.** How do you like the pizza?

_____   **8.** Where are the bananas?

_____   **9.** How many carrots do you want?

_____   **10.** Let's bake a cake for dessert!

a. We can't. There isn't any flour.

b. I think it's delicious.

c. Just a little.

d. They're on the counter.

e. I'm glad you like it.

f. Just a few.

g. We can't. There aren't any lemons.

h. I'm glad you like them.

i. It's in the cabinet.

j. I think they're delicious.

L LISTENING

Listen and put a check (✓) under the correct picture.

   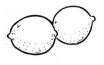

1. _____   ✓   **2.** _____   _____

3. _____   _____   **4.** _____   _____

5. _____   _____   **6.** _____   _____

7. _____   _____   **8.** _____   _____

9. _____   _____   **10.** _____   _____

Listen. Then clap and practice.

All. Not too much, just a little,

Not too many, just a few.

Not too much, just a little,

Not too many, just a few.

A. Would you like more chicken?

B. Just a little.

A. Would you like more carrots?

B. Just a few.

A. Would you like more gravy?

B. Just a little.

A. Would you like more mushrooms?

B. Just a few.

A. Would you like more salad?

B. Just a little.

A. Would you like more tomatoes?

B. Just a few.

A. Would you like more coffee?

B. Just a little.

A. Would you like more cookies?

B. Just a few.

All. Not too much, just a little.

Not too many, just a few.

Not too much, just a little.

Not too many, just a few.

A **SHOPPING LISTS**

bag	bunch	can	gallon	jar	loaf/loaves
bottle	box	dozen	head	pound	of

1. Jack is going to buy food at the supermarket.

Jack's Shopping List

a _____can_____ __of__ soup

a _____ _____ lettuce

a _____ _____ ketchup

a _____ _____ cheese

a _____ _____ flour

2. Jennifer is going to make breakfast for her parents.

Jennifer's Shopping List

a _____ _____ cereal

a _____ _____ jam

a _____ _____ bread

a _____ _____ bananas

a _____ _____ eggs

3. Mr. and Mrs. Baxter are going to have a birthday party for their daughter.

The Baxters' Shopping List

3 _____ _____ ice cream

2 _____ _____ cookies

2 _____ _____ grapes

3 _____ _____ meat

2 _____ _____ bread

4. What are YOU going to buy this week?

Your Shopping List

....

....

....

....

....

| bananas | cheese | cookies | ice cream | jam | onions |

1. Do we need anything from the supermarket?

Do we need anything else?

Yes. We need a jar of ___jam___.

Yes. We need a pint of _____

2. What do we need from the supermarket?

Do we need anything else?

We need a bunch of _____.

Yes. We need a box of _____

3. Do we need anything from the supermarket?

Do we need anything else?

Yes. We need a bag of _____.

Yes. We need a half a pound of _____.

C   LISTENING

Listen to the conversations. Put a check (✓) under the foods you hear.

1. __✓__   _____   __✓__   _____   __✓__

2. _____   _____   _____   _____   _____

3. _____   _____   _____   _____   _____

4. _____   _____   _____   _____   _____

Listen. Then clap and practice.

All.	We need	bread.
	Whole wheat	bread.
A.	How many	loaves do we need?
All.	Two.	

All.	We need	beans.
	Black	beans.
B.	How many	cans do we need?
All.	Three.	

All.	We need	rice.
	Brown	rice.
C.	How many	pounds do we need?
All.	Four.	

All.	We need	jam.
	Strawberry	jam.
D.	How many	jars do we need?
All.	Five.	

All.	We need	milk.
	Fresh	milk.
E.	How many	quarts do we need?
All.	Six.	

All.	We need	cash.
	We need	money.
F.	How much	money do we need?
All.	A lot!	

are	cost	does	loaf	money	of	quart
bread	costs	is	loaves	much	pound	right

1. A. How ___much___ does a _____ of milk _____?

   B. A _____ of _____ _____ two thirty-nine.

   A. Two dollars and thirty-nine cents?! That's a lot of _____!

   B. You're _____. Milk _____ very expensive this week.

2. A. How _____ does a _____ _____ bread cost?

   B. A _____ of _____ _____ one twenty-nine.

   A. Good! I'll take six _____, please.

   B. Six _____?! That's a lot _____ bread!

   A. I know. But _____ _____ very cheap this week!

3. A. How _____ _____ a _____ of apples cost?

   B. A _____ _____ apples _____ three sixty-five.

   A. Three sixty five?! That's too _____ money!

   B. You're right. Apples _____ very expensive today,

   but bananas _____ very cheap.

   A. That's nice. But how can I make an apple pie with bananas?!

F **LISTENING**

Listen and circle the price you hear.

1.	$1.95	($1.99)	4.	$25	25¢	7.	$3.13	$3.30
2.	$5	5¢	5.	$2.74	$2.47	8.	$1.15	$1.50
3.	$4.79	$9.47	6.	$6.60	$6.16	9.	$2.10	$21

1. A. What would you like for breakfast?
   B. Please give me an order of _____.
      a. cereal
      (b.) scrambled eggs

2. A. What would you like to drink?
   B. I want a glass of _____.
      a. milk
      b. coffee

3. A. What would you like for lunch?
   B. I want a bowl of _____.
      a. pancakes
      b. soup

4. A. Would you care for some dessert?
   B. Yes. I'd like a dish of _____.
      a. ice cream
      b. hot chocolate

5. A. What would you like?
   B. Please give me a cup of _____.
      a. tea
      b. cake

6. A. What would you like for dessert?
   B. I'd like a piece of _____.
      a. strawberries
      b. apple pie

H WHERE WOULD YOU LIKE TO GO FOR LUNCH?

are	glass	many	order
bowl	is	much	piece
cup	it	of	they
dish			

A. Where would you like to go for lunch?

B. Let's go to Carla's Cafe. Their spaghetti ___is___ ¹ out of this world and _____ ² isn't expensive. I had an _____ _____ ³ ⁴ spaghetti there last week for a dollar ninety-five.

A. I don't really want to go to Carla's Cafe. Their spaghetti _____ ⁵ very good, but you can't get any chocolate milk. I like to have a _____ ⁶ of chocolate milk with my lunch.

B. How about The Pancake Place? Their pancakes _____ ⁷ fantastic, and _____ ⁸ aren't expensive. An _____ _____ ⁹ ¹⁰ pancakes costs two sixty-nine.

A. I really don't like The Pancake Place. The pancakes _____ ¹¹ tasty, but their salad _____ ¹² terrible! It has too _____ ¹³ lettuce and too _____ ¹⁴ onions.

B. Well, how about Rita's Restaurant? Their desserts are wonderful. You can get a delicious _____ _____ ¹⁵ ¹⁶ pie, a _____ _____ ¹⁷ ¹⁸ strawberries, or a _____ _____ ¹⁹ ²⁰ ice cream.

A. I know. But their hot chocolate _____ ²¹ very bad. I like to have a _____ _____ ²² ²³ hot chocolate with my dessert.

B. Wait a minute! I know where we can go for lunch. Let's go to YOUR house!

GRAMMARRAP: *Grocery List*

Listen. Then clap and practice.

We need a loaf of — bread
And a jar of — jam,
A box of — cookies
And a pound of — ham.
A bottle of — ketchup,
A pound of — cheese,
A dozen — eggs,
And a can of — peas.
A head of — lettuce,
Half a pound of — rice,
A bunch of — bananas,
And a bag of — ice.

a loaf of bread
a jar of jam
a box of cookies
a pound of ham
a bottle of ketchup

 GRAMMARRAP: *What Would You Like to Have?*

Listen. Then clap and practice.

A. What would you like to order?
What would you like to have?

B. An order of chicken, a dish of potatoes,
A large green salad with a lot of tomatoes.
A bowl of soup, an order of rice,
And a glass of soda with a lot of ice.

A. And what would you like for dessert?

B. Nothing, thanks. I'm not very hungry!

K WHAT'S THE WORD?

1. Slice the ⬚honey (carrots) .

2. Cut up the ⬚oranges / salt .

3. Chop up the ⬚flour / nuts .

4. Pour in the ⬚water / potatoes .

5. Slice the ⬚baking soda / apples .

6. Pour it into the mixing ⬚bowl / recipe .

7. ⬚Mix in / Put the raisins.

8. ⬚Add / Cook for two hours.

L WHAT'S THE RECIPE?

⬚ a little   a few

Millie's Tomato Sauce

1. Put _____a little_____ butter into a pan.

2. Chop up _____ onions.

3. Cut up _____ mushrooms and _____ cheese.

4. Slice _____ tomatoes.

5. Add _____ salt and _____ pepper.

6. Cook for _____ minutes.

M LISTENING

Listen and choose the correct word to complete the sentence.

1. a. onions
   b. water

2. a. cheese
   b. nuts

3. a. oranges
   b. baking soda

4. a. salt
   b. raisins

5. a. tomato
   b. potatoes

6. a. pepper
   b. mushrooms

A. Fill in the blanks.

Ex. a ___quart___
of milk

1. a _____
of bananas

2. a _____
of soup

3. a _____
of onions

4. a _____
of pie

5. 2 _____
of cereal

6. 2 _____
of bread

B. Circle the correct answers.

Ex. Yogurt (is) / are cheap today.

1. I eat too much / many cookies.

2. She ate so much / many cake that
she has a stomachache.

3. What do you like / like to do on the
weekend?

4. How much / many does a bowl of
strawberries cost?

5. Would you care for a little / few grapes?

I bought it / them this morning, and

it's / they're very fresh.

6. This / These rice is / are delicious. May I

have a little / few more?

C. Complete the sentences.

Ex. Janet watches TV every Friday.

___She watched___ TV last Friday.

___She's going to watch___ TV next Friday.

1. Alan drives to the mall every week.

He _____ to the mall last week.

_____
to the mall next week.

2. I go on vacation every year.

I _____ on vacation last year.

_____
on vacation next year.

3. We play baseball every Saturday.

We _____ baseball last Saturday.

_____ baseball next Saturday.

4. My sister writes letters to her friends every weekend.

She _____ letters to her friends last weekend.

_____ letters to her friends next weekend.

5. Ed makes pancakes every morning.

He _____ pancakes yesterday morning.

_____ pancakes tomorrow morning.

D. Complete the sentences.

Ex. Last year my parents gave me a sweater for my birthday.

This year ___*they're going to give me*___ a jacket.

1. Last year Tom gave his girlfriend flowers.

This year _____

_____ candy.

2. Last year Sue gave her husband a CD player.

This year _____

_____ a briefcase.

3. Last year we gave our parents a cell phone.

This year _____

_____ a computer.

"I'm sorry, but there _____ any."

Ex.
| isn't |
| (aren't) |

3.
| isn't |
| aren't |

1.
| isn't |
| aren't |

4.
| isn't |
| aren't |

2.
| isn't |
| aren't |

5.
| isn't |
| aren't |

A FOOD SHOPPING

Read the article on student book page 27 and answer the questions.

STUDENT BOOK
PAGES **27–28**

1. In the past, people shopped _____.
   a. at supermarkets
   b. online
   c. at open markets
   d. at wholesale stores

2. Today people don't have to shop every day because _____.
   a. they have refrigerators
   b. they have busy lives
   c. many stores sell food at low prices
   d. it's difficult to keep food fresh

3. *Enormous* in paragraph 3 means very _____.
   a. cheap
   b. large
   c. modern
   d. busy

4. People shop at wholesale stores because _____.
   a. the stores deliver food to their homes
   b. the food is always very fresh
   c. they don't like large stores
   d. they want to save money

5. Open markets are always _____.
   a. outside
   b. in the city
   c. open 24 hours a day
   d. small

6. Today most people shop for food _____.
   a. almost every day
   b. on the Internet
   c. once or twice a week
   d. every day

7. *People still shop in little food stores* means _____.
   a. they like to shop in little food stores
   b. they can't shop in little food stores
   c. they rarely shop in little food stores
   d. they shopped in little food stores in the past, and they shop in them now

8. The main idea of this article is that _____.
   a. refrigerators keep food fresh
   b. people shop for food in different ways
   c. today's stores sell food at low prices
   d. it's convenient to shop on the Internet

B BUILD YOUR VOCABULARY! Crossword

Across

2.

3.

4.

7.

8.

Down

1.

5.

6.

Look at the Fact File on student book page 27 and answer the questions.

1. Hens produce _____.
   a. rice
   b. cocoa
   c. eggs
   d. chocolate

2. According to the fact file, the world produces more than _____ eggs a day.
   a. 200,000,000,000
   b. 2,000,000,000
   c. 200,000,000
   d. 20,000,000

3. It takes 8,818 tons of cocoa beans to make _____ chocolate bars.
   a. 7,000,000
   b. 70,000,000
   c. 700,000,000
   d. 7,000,000,000

4. The world produces _____ tons of rice a day.
   a. 1,000,006
   b. 1,000,600
   c. 1,000,060
   d. 1,600,000

5. Cyprus is a very large _____.
   a. city
   b. pyramid
   c. island
   d. omelet

6. The world produces more than a million and a half _____ every day.
   a. tons of cocoa beans
   b. tons of rice
   c. tons of chocolate bars
   d. tons of cocoa bars

7. The world produces _____ pounds of cocoa beans every day. (There are 2,000 pounds in a ton.)
   a. 8,818
   b. 17,636
   c. 700,000,000
   d. 17,636,000

8. According to the Fact File, the world produces more than _____ in a week.
   a. 14 billion eggs
   b. 70,000 tons of cocoa
   c. 14 million tons of rice
   d. 7 billion chocolate bars

Match the "can do" statement and the correct sentence.

____ 1. I can tell about favorite activities.

____ 2. I can ask about past activities.

____ 3. I can ask about future plans.

____ 4. I can compliment about food.

____ 5. I can express gratitude.

____ 6. I can get someone's attention.

____ 7. I can give instructions.

____ 8. I can ask for a recommendation.

____ 9. I can make a recommendation.

____ 10. I can agree with someone.

a. What are you going to do next weekend?

b. Thanks.

c. I suggest our chicken soup.

d. Chop up a few onions.

e. I like to go hiking.

f. You're right.

g. What do you recommend?

h. Your cake is delicious.

i. What did you do yesterday?

j. Excuse me.

STUDENT BOOK
PAGES **29–38**

1. A. Will you be back soon?

B. Yes, _____I will_____. _____I'll_____

_____be back_____ in half an hour.

2. A. Will the game begin soon?

B. Yes, _____. _____

_____ in ten minutes.

3. A. Will Henry return soon?

B. Yes, _____. _____

_____ in a week.

4. A. Will we be ready soon?

B. Yes, _____. _____

_____ in a little while.

5. A. Will Grandma and Grandpa arrive soon?

B. Yes, _____. _____

_____ in 15 or 20 minutes.

6. A. Will the storm end soon?

B. Yes, _____. _____

_____ in a few hours.

7. A. Will Kate be here soon?

B. Yes, _____. _____

_____ in a few minutes.

8. A. Will you get out soon?

B. Yes, _____. _____

_____ in a month.

1. Do you think Barbara ___will___ move to a new apartment soon?

I don't know. Maybe ___she___ ___will___, and maybe ___she___ ___won't___.

2. Do you think Robert _____ like his new job?

I don't know. Maybe _____, and maybe _____.

3. Do you think _____ drive to the beach this weekend?

I don't know. Maybe I _____, and maybe _____.

4. Do you think _____ be a famous scientist some day?

I don't know. Maybe you _____, and maybe _____.

5. Do you think _____ snow a lot this winter?

I don't know. Maybe _____, and maybe _____.

6. Do you think _____ _____ be a lot of traffic today?

I don't know. Maybe _____, and maybe _____.

7. Do you think you and Roger _____ get married soon?

I don't know. Maybe _____, and maybe _____.

8. Do you think the guests _____ like the fruitcake?

I don't know. Maybe _____, and maybe _____.

	Yes!	*No!*

1. What will Charlie bake for the party?

Maybe _____ he'll _____

_____ bake _____ cookies.

I'm sure _____ he _____

_____ won't bake _____ a cake.

2. What will Mom order at the restaurant?

Maybe _____

_____ a sandwich.

I'm sure _____

_____ a pizza.

3. Where will your parents go this evening?

Maybe _____

_____ to a movie.

I'm sure _____

_____ to a party.

4. What will you get for your birthday?

Maybe _____

_____ a sweater.

I'm sure _____

_____ a cell phone.

5. When will the train arrive?

Maybe _____

_____ in an hour.

I'm sure _____

_____ on time.

6. When will we finish our English book?

Maybe _____

_____ it in a few months.

I'm sure _____

_____ it next week.

D **LISTENING**

Listen and circle the words you hear.

1. (won't) / (want to)
2. won't / want to
3. won't / want to
4. won't / want to
5. won't / want to
6. won't / want to
7. won't / want to
8. won't / want to

E **DIFFERENT OPINIONS**

1. I think the weather will be nice tomorrow. Everybody else thinks _____ it'll be _____ bad.

2. My wife thinks the guests will arrive on time. I think _____ late.

3. I think our daughter will be a lawyer. My husband thinks _____ an architect.

4. My parents think my brother Bob will buy a bicycle. I think _____ a motorcycle.

5. I think we'll have a good time at the party. My husband thinks _____ a terrible time.

Listen. Then clap and practice.

A.   I'll   remember.

B.   Are you   sure?

A.   Don't   worry.   I'll remember.   You'll see.

A.   He'll   do it.

B.   Are you   sure?

A.   Don't   worry.   He'll do it.   You'll see.

A.   She'll   call you.

B.   Are you   sure?

A.   Don't   worry.   She'll call you.   You'll see.

A.   It'll be   ready.

B.   Are you   sure?

A.   Don't   worry.   It'll be ready.   You'll see.

A.   We'll   be there.

B.   Are you   sure?

A.   Don't   worry.   We'll be there.   You'll see.

A.   They'll   get there.

B.   Are you   sure?

A.   Don't   worry.   They'll get there.   You'll see.

1. A. What's Bruno going to make for breakfast this morning?

   B. _____He might make eggs_____, or

   _____he might make pancakes_____.

2. A. What time is Sally going to get up tomorrow morning on her day off?

   B. _____, or

   _____.

3. A. When are your children going to clean their bedroom?

   B. _____, or

   _____.

4. A. What are you going to give your parents for their anniversary?

   B. _____, or

   _____.

5. A. What are you and your friends going to watch on TV tonight?

   B. _____, or

   _____.

6. A. Where are Mr. and Mrs. Martinez going to go for their vacation?

   B. _____, or

   _____.

7. A. Tell me, what are you going to do this weekend?

   B. _____, or

   _____.

8. A. What's Arthur going to name his new cat?

   B. _____, or

   _____.

H ▸ BE CAREFUL!

1. Don't stand there!
   (a.) You might get hit.
   b. You might watch.

2. Put on your safety glasses!
   a. You might hurt your ears.
   b. You might hurt your eyes.

3. Don't touch those wires!
   a. You might get a shock.
   b. You might get cold.

4. Don't touch that machine!
   a. You might get hurt.
   b. You might get a helmet.

5. Watch your step!
   a. You might finish.
   b. You might fall.

6. Put on your helmet!
   a. You might hurt your back.
   b. You might hurt your head.

I ▸ LOUD AND CLEAR

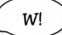
W!

winter Wendy walk weather work

1. ___Wendy___ doesn't like to ___walk___ to ___work___ in the ___winter___ when the ___weather___ is bad.

wet walk waiter won't waitress

2. The _____ and the _____ _____ _____ there. The floor is _____!

wife wash Walter windows want weekend

3. _____ and his _____ _____ to _____ their _____ this _____.

wasn't we water wanted warm

4. _____ _____ to go swimming, but the _____ _____ _____.

Activity Workbook   **35**

break her leg	fall asleep	get fat	have a terrible time	rain
catch a cold	get a backache	get seasick	look terrible	step on her feet
drown	get a sunburn	get sick	miss our bus	

1. Jennifer won't go skating because

   she's afraid she might

   break her leg .

2. George won't go to the beach because

   _____

   _____ .

3. I won't go swimming because

   _____

   _____ .

4. We won't have lunch with you because

   _____

   _____ .

5. My mother and father won't go on the roller

   coaster because _____

   _____ .

6. Brian won't go dancing with Brenda

   because _____

   _____ .

7. We won't go to a play because

   _____

   _____ .

8. I won't go to Patty's party because

   _____

   _____ .

9. Barry won't carry those boxes because

_____

_____ .

10. Sally won't go sailing because

_____

_____ .

11. I won't eat dessert because

_____

_____ .

12. Helen won't take a walk in the park because

_____

_____ .

13. We won't wash our clothes today because

_____

_____ .

14. Fred won't get a short haircut because

_____

_____ .

K LISTENING

Listen and choose the correct answer.

1. (a.) He doesn't want to go on the roller coaster.
   b. He doesn't want to go to the doctor.

2. a. She doesn't want to go skiing.
   b. She doesn't want to go to the movies.

3. a. He doesn't want to go to a play.
   b. He doesn't want to go dancing.

4. a. She doesn't want to go skiing.
   b. She doesn't want to stay home.

5. a. He doesn't want to read a book.
   b. He doesn't want to take a walk in the park.

6. a. He doesn't want to go swimming.
   b. He doesn't want to go dancing.

7. a. She doesn't want to go skating.
   b. She doesn't want to go sailing.

8. a. He doesn't want to go to the library.
   b. He doesn't want to go to the beach.

9. a. She doesn't want to go to the party.
   b. She doesn't want to eat dinner.

10. a. He doesn't want to get a short haircut.
    b. He doesn't want to buy a small dog.

Listen. Then clap and practice.

A.   When is he going to   leave?

B.   He might leave at   noon.

C.   He might leave on   Monday.

D.   He might leave in   June.

A.   Where is he going to   go?

B.   He might go to   Spain.

C.   He might go to   Texas.

D.   He might go to   Maine.

A.   How is he going to   get there?

B.   He might go by   train.

C.   He might take the   bus.

D.   He might take a   plane.

A.   Who is he going to   go with?

B.   He might go with   Ed.

C.   He might go with   Peter.

D.   He might go with   Fred.

A.   What's he going to   do there?

B.   He might see the   zoo.

C.   He might take some   pictures.

D.   He might write to   you.

Listen and fill in the words to the song. Then listen again and sing along.

cake	decide	go	her	make	Mexico	sweater	wide

I want to cook some dinner.

I don't know what to ___make___ 1.

I might make stew. I might make eggs.

I might just bake a _____ 2.

I really don't know what to cook.

The choices are so _____ 3.

I might cook this. I might cook that.

I really can't _____ 4.

I'm planning my vacation.

I don't know where to _____ 5.

I might see France. I might see Spain.

I might see _____ 6.

I really don't know where to go.

The choices are so _____ 7.

I might go here. I might go there.

I really can't _____ 8.

I'm buying Mom a present.

I don't know what to get _____ 9.

I might buy gloves. I might buy boots.

I might get her a _____ 10.

I really don't know what to get.

The choices are so _____ 11.

I might get this. I might get that.

I really can't _____ 12.

A OLD AND NEW

STUDENT BOOK
PAGES **39–48**

1. Henry's old sofa was soft. His new sofa is _____ softer _____.

2. Nancy's old briefcase was light. Her new briefcase is _____.

3. Bob's old living room was large. His new living room is _____.

4. My old recipe for chili was hot. My new recipe is _____.

5. My old boss was friendly. My new boss is _____.

6. Our old neighborhood was safe. Our new neighborhood is _____.

7. Linda's old cell phone was small. Her new cell phone is _____.

8. Grandpa's old sports car was fancy. His new sports car is _____.

9. Cathy's old mittens were warm. Her new mittens are _____.

10. Billy's old school was big. His new school is _____.

11. My old job was easy. My new job is _____.

12. Our old neighbors were nice. Our new neighbors are _____.

13. Richard's old watch was cheap. His new watch is _____.

14. Dr. Green's old office was ugly. His new office is _____.

B WHAT'S THE WORD?

 Tima   Jim

1. A. Is Tim's hair short?

   B. Yes, but Jim's hair is _____ shorter _____.

2. A. Is Charlie's cat cute?

   B. Yes, but his dog is _____.

 Barbara   Betty

3. A. Is Debbie's dog fat?

   B. Yes, but her cat is _____.

4. A. Is Barbara busy?

   B. Yes, but Betty is _____.

40   **Activity Workbook**

C THEY'RE DIFFERENT

1. Paul's parrot is talkative, but Paula's parrot is _____ more talkative _____ .

2. Your roommate is interesting, but my roommate is _____ .

3. Sam's suit is attractive, but Stanley's suit is _____ .

4. Shirley's shoes are comfortable, but her sister's shoes are _____ .

5. George is intelligent, but his brother is _____ .

6. My daughter's hair is long, but my son's hair is _____ .

7. Last winter was cold, but this winter is _____ .

8. William is thin, but his father is _____ .

9. My children are healthy, but my doctor's children are _____ .

10. John's computer is powerful, but Jane's computer is _____ .

11. Barbara's boyfriend is handsome, but her father is _____ .

12. My teeth are white, but my dentist's teeth are _____ .

13. Our neighbor's yard is beautiful, but our yard is _____ .

D WHAT'S THE WORD?

1. A. This meatloaf is delicious.
    B. It's very good, but my mother's meatloaf

    is _____ more delicious _____ .

2. A. Chicken is good for you.
    B. I know. But everybody says that fish

    is _____ for you.

3. A. This necklace is very expensive.
    B. You're right. But that necklace

    is _____ .

4. A. You're very energetic!
    B. Yes, I am. But my wife is _____

    _____ .

Across

4. My upstairs neighbor is friendly, but my downstairs neighbor is _____.
7. Their baby is cute, but my baby is _____.
8. Betty's blue dress is pretty, but her green dress is _____.
11. This bicycle is fast, but that bicycle is _____.
12. My old apartment was large, but my new apartment is _____.
13. Your dishwasher is quiet, but my dishwasher is _____.

Down

1. Our old rug was soft, but our new rug is _____.
2. Yesterday it was warm, but today it's _____.
3. Their new house is small, but their old house was _____.
4. Tom's new tie is fancy, but his son's tie is _____.
5. My old tennis racket was light, but my new tennis racket is_____.
6. Bananas were cheap last week, but this week they're _____.
9. The chili we ate last week was hot, but this chili is _____.
10. This picture is ugly, but that picture is ____.

F LISTENING

Listen and choose the correct words to complete the sentences.

1. a. cooler
   b. cuter

2. a. smaller
   b. taller

3. a. more handsome
   b. more attractive

4. a. nicer
   b. lighter

5. a. fatter
   b. faster

6. a. friendlier
   b. fancier

7. a. more interesting
   b. more intelligent

8. a. bigger
   b. busier

LET'S COMPARE!

cheap	delicious	fancy	small	talented	talkative

1.   John's tie   Jack's tie

_____Jack's tie is fancier than_____

_____John's tie._____.

2.   the computer   the printer

_____

_____.

3.   the chicken   the meatballs

_____

_____.

4.   Dick   Rick

_____

_____.

5.   Carla's car   Carol's car

_____

_____.

6.   Fred   Frank

_____

_____.

GRAMMARRAP: *Honey Is Sweeter Than Sugar*

Listen. Then clap and practice.

Honey is	sweeter than	sugar.		Peaches are	softer than	apples.
Coffee is	stronger than	tea.		Pepper is	hotter than	rice.
Hours are	longer than	minutes.		Pears are	bigger than	lemons.
Thirty is	larger than three.			Nothing is	colder than	ice.

Activity Workbook   43

Listen and circle the correct answer.

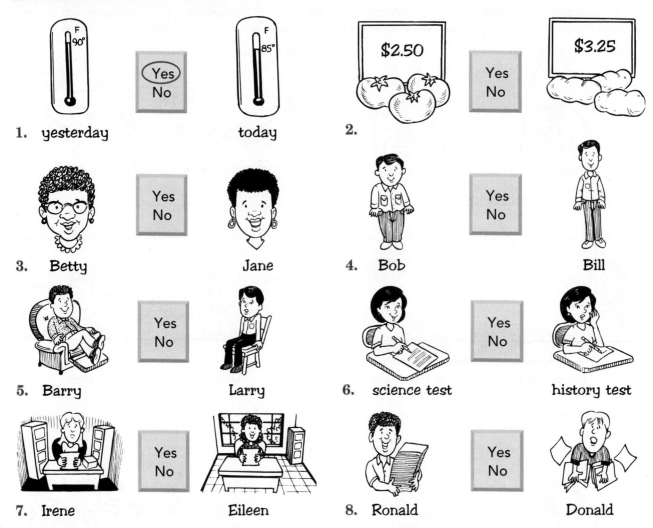

1.   yesterday   today

2.

3.   Betty   Jane

4.   Bob   Bill

5.   Barry   Larry

6.   science test   history test

7.   Irene   Eileen

8.   Ronald   Donald

J GRAMMARRAP: *I Can't Decide*

Listen. Then clap and practice.

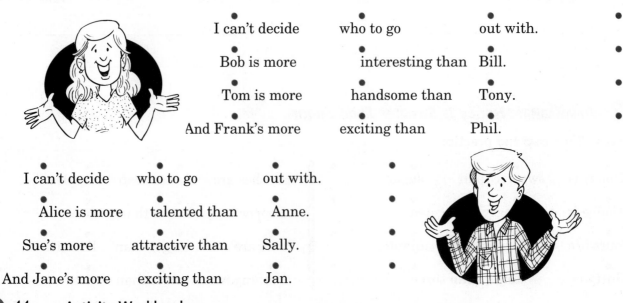

I can't decide   who to go   out with.

Bob is more   interesting than Bill.

Tom is more   handsome than   Tony.

And Frank's more   exciting than   Phil.

I can't decide   who to go   out with.

Alice is more   talented than   Anne.

Sue's more   attractive than   Sally.

And Jane's more   exciting than   Jan.

K WHAT SHOULD THEY DO?

call the dentist	fire him	rent a video
call the police	hire her	plant some flowers

1. My garden looks terrible!

You should plant some flowers.

2. Harvey has a very bad toothache!

_____

3. My husband and I want to see a movie tonight.

_____

4. A thief stole my daughter's new bicycle!

_____

5. The people at the Ace company think that Jennifer is capable and talented.

_____

6. Ms. Hunter is upset because her secretary falls asleep at work every day.

_____

L GRAMMARRAP: *Should They . . . ?*

Listen. Then clap and practice.

A. Should he   call or should he   write?

B.   He should call   tomorrow   night.

A. Should I   keep it or give it   back?

B. You should wear it or give it to   Jack.

A. Should I   stay or   should I   go?

B. Don't ask me.   I don't know.

Activity Workbook   **45**

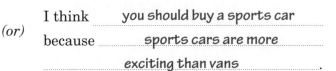

useful   exciting

1. Should I buy a van or a sports car?

I think ____ *you should buy a van*
because ____ *vans are more useful than*   *(or)*   I think ____ *you should buy a sports car*
____ *sports cars* .   because ____ *sports cars are more*
____ *exciting than vans* .

safe   fast

quiet   beautiful

2. Should she buy a bicycle or a motorcycle?

I think ____
because ____
____ .

3. Should we move to Weston or Easton?

I think ____
because ____
____ .

warm   fancy

talented   honest

4. Should he buy the fur hat or the leather hat?

I think ____
because ____
____ .

5. Should I vote for Alan Lane or George Gray?

I think ____
because ____
____ .

Mr. Hall   Mr. Hill
nice   capable

Patty   Pam
interesting   intelligent

6. Should we hire Mr. Hall or Mr. Hill?

I think ____
because ____
____ .

7. Should he go out with Patty or Pam?

I think ____
because ____
____ .

WHAT'S THE WORD?

mine	his	hers	ours	yours	theirs

1. A. Is this Michael's cell phone?

   B. No. It isn't _____ his _____.

2. A. Are these your safety glasses?

   B. No. They aren't _____.

3. A. Is this your sister's violin?

   B. No. It isn't _____.

4. A. Is that Mr. and Mrs. Garcia's van?

   B. No. It isn't _____.

5. A. Is this my recipe for fruitcake?

   B. No. It isn't _____.

6. A. Are these your son's sneakers?

   B. No. They aren't _____.

7.
Is that your car?

No. It isn't _____.

WHAT'S THE WORD?

1. You know, my parents aren't as sympathetic as your parents.

   Really? I think ((yours) your) are much more sympathetic than (my   mine).

2. Robert's cookies aren't as delicious as his sister's cookies.

   Really? I think (him   his) are much more delicious than (her   hers).

3. Our computer isn't as fast as their computer.

   Really? I think (ours   their) is much faster than (theirs   them).

4. My pronunciation isn't as good as your pronunciation.

   Don't be ridiculous! (Your   Yours) is much better than (mine   my).

5. Jane's briefcase isn't as attractive as her husband's briefcase.

   Really? I think (her   hers) is much more attractive than (him   his).

P DIFFERENT, BUT OKAY

1. My neighborhood (quiet) _____isn't as quiet as_____ your neighborhood, but it's much (interesting) _____more interesting_____.

2. Susan's sofa (fashionable) _____ her sister's sofa, but it's much (comfortable) _____.

3. These apartments (modern) _____ our apartment, but they're much (large) _____.

4. George's car (powerful) _____ Jack's car, but it's much (reliable) _____.

5. The weather in our city (warm) _____ the weather in your city, but it's much (sunny) _____.

6. My parents (talkative) _____ my cousin's parents, but they're much (understanding) _____.

7. The movie we rented last weekend wasn't (exciting) _____ this movie, but it was much (good) _____.

Q YOU'RE RIGHT

1. A. Ken's tie isn't as attractive as Len's tie.

   B. You're right. Len's tie is _____more_____
   _____attractive than Ken's tie_____.

2. A. Donald isn't as nice as Ronald.

   B. You're right. Ronald is _____
   _____.

3. A. Larry isn't as lazy as his brother.

   B. You're right. Larry's brother is _____
   _____.

4. A. English isn't as difficult as Russian.

   B. You're right. Russian is _____
   _____.

5. A. Julie's office isn't as big as Judy's office.

   B. You're right. Judy's office is _____
   _____.

6. A. My son isn't as talkative as your son.

   B. You're right. My son is _____
   _____.

Listen. Then clap and practice.

Where's my   ticket?

Who has   mine?

I don't   want to

stand in   line.

Who has   hers?

Who has   his?

I wonder   where

my ticket   is!

He has   his.

I have   mine.

She has   hers.

Everything's   fine!

S **GRAMMARRAP:** *His Job Is Easy*

Listen. Then clap and practice.

His job is   easy.

Hers is,   too.

Mine's a more   difficult   job to   do.

His job's as   simple

As A B   C.

Mine   requires a   P H   D.

T WHO SHOULD WE HIRE?

A. Do you think we should hire Mr. Blake or Mr. Maxwell?

B. I'm not sure. Mr. Blake isn't as (lively) _____ *lively* _____ [1]

as Mr. Maxwell, but he's much (smart) _____ [2].

A. I agree. Mr. Blake is very smart, but in my opinion,

Mr. Maxwell is (talented) _____ [3] than
Mr. Blake.

B. Well, perhaps Mr. Blake isn't as (talented) _____ [4] as

Mr. Maxwell, but I think he's probably (honest) _____ [5].

A. Do you really think so?

B. Yes. I think Mr. Blake is much (good) _____ [6] for the job.
We should hire him.

A. Do you think we should hire Ms. Taylor or Ms. Tyler?

B. I'm not sure. Ms. Tyler isn't as (friendly) _____ [7]

as Ms. Taylor, but I think she's much (intelligent) _____

_____ [8].

A. But Ms. Taylor is (talkative) _____ [9]

and (polite) _____ [10] than Ms. Tyler.

B. That's true. But I think Ms. Tyler is (capable) _____

_____ [11] than Ms. Taylor. I think we should hire her.

A. Do you think we should hire Mario or Victor?

B. I don't know. Mario's meatballs are (good) _____ [12]

than Victor's, but his desserts aren't as (delicious)

_____ [13] as Victor's desserts.

A. That's true. But Mario's vegetable stew is (interesting)

_____ [14] than Victor's. Also, Mario is

much (fast) _____ [15] than Victor. He's also

(nice) _____ [16] than Victor.

B. You're right. I think we should hire Mario.

1. A. I think Alice is very bright.

   B. She certainly is. She's _____the_____

   ___brightest___ student in our class.

2. A. Your brother Tom is very neat.

   B. He certainly is. He's _____

   _____ person I know.

3. A. Our upstairs neighbors are very nice.

   B. I agree. They're _____
   people in the building.

4. A. This dress is very fancy.

   B. I know. It's _____
   dress in the store.

5. A. I think Nancy is very friendly.

   B. I agree. She's _____
   person in our office.

6. A. Timothy is very quiet.

   B. I know. He's _____
   boy in the school.

7. A. Is their new baby cute?

   B. In my opinion, she's _____

   _____ baby girl in
   the hospital.

8. A. That dog is very big.

   B. It certainly is. It's _____

   _____ dog in the
   neighborhood.

9. A. Your cousin Steven is very sloppy.

   B. He certainly is. He's _____

   _____ person I know.

10. A. Morton Miller is very mean.

    B. I agree. He's _____

    _____ man in town.

boring	generous	interesting	patient	smart	talented
energetic	honest	noisy	polite	stubborn	

1. Jessica sings, dances, and plays the guitar. She's very _____ talented _____.

   In fact, she's _____ the most talented _____ person I know.

2. Mr. Bates gives very expensive gifts to his friends. He's very _____.

   In fact, he's _____ person I know.

3. My Aunt Louise jogs every day before work. She's very _____.

   In fact, she's _____ person I know.

4. Marvin always says "Thank you" and "You're welcome." He's very _____.

   In fact, he's _____ person I know.

5. Samantha always knows the answers to all the questions. She's very _____.

   In fact, she's _____ person I know.

6. Edward isn't reading a very exciting novel. It's very _____.

   In fact, it's _____ book in his house.

7. Dr. Chen never gets angry. She's very _____.

   In fact, she's _____ person I know.

8. Mayor Jones always says what he thinks. He's very _____.

   In fact, he's _____ person I know.

9. My next-door neighbor plays loud music after midnight. He's very _____.

   In fact, he's _____ person I know.

10. I'm never bored in my English class. My English teacher is very _____.

    In fact, she's _____ person I know.

11. My brother-in-law is always sure he's right. He's very _____.

    In fact, he's _____ person I know.

C WORLDBUY.COM

WorldBuy.com is a very popular website on the Internet. People like to shop there because they can find wonderful products from around the world at very low prices.

1. *(attractive!)* Julie is buying a briefcase from Italy because she thinks that Italian briefcases are _____the most attractive_____ briefcases in the world.

2. *(soft!)* David is buying leather boots from Spain because he thinks that Spanish boots are _____ boots in the world.

3. *(elegant!)* Francine is buying an evening gown from Paris because she thinks that French evening gowns are _____ gowns in the world.

4. *(modern!)* Mr. and Mrs. Chang are buying a sofa from Sweden because they think that Swedish furniture is _____ furniture in the world.

5. *(warm!)* Victor is buying a fur hat from Russia because he thinks that Russian hats are _____ hats in the world.

6. *(good!)* Brenda is buying a sweater from England because she thinks that English sweaters are _____ sweaters in the world.

7. *(reliable!)* Michael is buying a watch from Switzerland because he thinks that Swiss watches are _____ watches in the world.

8. *(beautiful!)* Mr. and Mrs. Rivera are buying a rug from China because they think that Chinese rugs are _____ rugs in the world.

9. *(delicious!)* Nancy is buying coffee from Brazil because she thinks that Brazilian coffee is _____ in the world.

10. *(............!)* I'm buying .... from .... because I think that ....s is/are .... in the world.

Listen. Then clap and practice.

A.   What do you   think about   Kirk?

B.   He's the friendliest   person at   work!

A.   What do you   think about   Flo?

B.   She's the most patient   person I   know!

A.   What do you   think about   Pete?

B.   He's the nicest   boy on the   street!

A.   What do you   think about   Kate?

B.   She's the most talented   teacher in the   state!

A.   What do you   think about   Bob?

B.   He's the laziest   guy on the   job!

A.   What do you   think about   Frank?

B.   He's the most polite   teller at the   bank!

A.   What do you   think about   Nellie?

B.   She's the fastest   waitress at the   deli!

A.   What do you   think about this   kitty?

B.   It's the ugliest   cat in the   city!

1. A. How do you like your new BMB van, Mr. Lopez?

    B. It's very powerful. It's much ____more____

    _____powerful_____ than my old van.

    A. That's because the BMB van is _____

    _____the most powerful_____ van in the world!

2. A. How do you like your Suny video camera, Mrs. Park?

    B. It's very lightweight. It's much _____

    _____ than my old video camera.

    A. That's because the Suny video camera is _____

    _____ video camera in the world!

3. A. How do you like your new Inkflo printer, Ted?

    B. It's very efficient. It's much _____

    _____ than my old printer.

    A. That's because the Inkflo printer is _____

    _____ printer in the world!

4. A. How do you like your Panorama fax machine, Jane?

    B. It's very dependable. It's much _____

    _____ than my old fax machine.

    A. That's because the Panorama fax machine is _____

    _____ fax machine in the world!

5. A. How do you like your new Ever-Lite Flashlight, Henry?

    B. It's very bright. It's much _____ than the
        flashlight I usually use.

    A. That's because the Ever-Lite Flashlight is _____

    _____ flashlight in the world!

F LISTENING 🔊

Listen and circle the words you hear.

1. (more comfortable)   the most comfortable   6. sloppier   the sloppiest

2. the best   the worst   7. the worst   the best

3. more energetic   the most energetic   8. lazier   lazy

4. cheap   cheaper   9. meaner   mean

5. the most important   more important   10. more honest   the most honest

G PUZZLE

| boring | comfortable | delicious | good | honest | polite | safe | sloppy | small | ugly |

Across

2. Some people don't like this cereal. But I
   disagree. I think it's _____ cereal in
   the world.

5. Even though Harry's Restaurant is the
   most popular restaurant in town, it isn't
   _____.

6. This is my favorite chair. That's because
   it's _____ chair in the house.

7. My house isn't very big. In fact, it's
   _____ house on the street.

8. Their old neighborhood was dangerous,
   but their new neighborhood is _____
   neighborhood in the city.

Down

1. Even though the salespeople at Ace Used
   Cars are the most helpful in town, they
   aren't _____.

2. My son isn't very neat. In my opinion,
   he's _____ person in our family.

3. I think golf is very interesting. But my
   wife disagrees. She thinks it's _____
   game in the world.

4. Charles is never rude. In fact, he's
   _____ boy in the school.

6. Emily's cat isn't very pretty. In my
   opinion, it's _____ cat in town!

● **56**   **Activity Workbook**

H **LOUD AND CLEAR** **r!**

Fill in the words. Then read the sentences aloud.

worst	program	Andrew
terrible		actor

1. ___Andrew___ is the ___worst___

   ___actor___ on this ___terrible___

   TV ___program___!

recipe	Carla's	fruitcake
recommend		better

2. I _____ _____

   _____ for _____.

   It's _____ than yours.

energetic	friendlier	Robert
more		brother

3. _____ is _____

   and _____ _____

   than his _____ Richard.

newspaper	writes	reads
Rita		morning

4. _____ _____ the _____

   every _____, and she

   _____ letters every afternoon.

perfume	birthday	sister
Ronald		thirtieth

5. _____ gave his _____

   flowers and _____ for her

   _____ _____.

powerful	bigger	more
neighbor's		car

6. My _____ is _____ and

   _____ _____ than my

   _____ car.

✔ CHECK-UP TEST: Chapters 4–6

A. Complete the sentences.

Ex. Will you be ready soon?

Yes, __I will__. __I'll__
be ready in a few minutes.

Ex. Will your brother get home soon?

No, __he won't__. He's at a baseball
game tonight.

1. Will the storm end soon?

Yes, _____. _____
end in a few hours.

2. Will Carol and Dave be in the office today?

No, _____. They're on vacation.

3. Will you return soon?

Yes, _____. _____
return in a little while.

4. Will Jane be in school tomorrow?

No, _____. She has a bad
cold.

5. Will you and Ray get out of work soon?

Yes, _____. _____
get out in half an hour.

B. Circle the correct answers.

1. I'm not going to fix that wire. I'm

afraid I | might | get a shock.
          | should |

2. What do you think?

| Might | I order the chicken or the fish?
| Should |

3. When I grow up I | might | be a
                     | should |

dentist, or I | might | be a doctor.
               | should |

4. It's going to rain. You | might | take
                            | should |

your umbrella.

C. Complete the conversations.

Ex. A. Are these Maria's gloves?

B. No. They aren't _____hers_____.

1. A. Is that your video camera?

B. No. It isn't _____.

2. A. Is that your son's computer?

B. No. It isn't _____.

3. A. Is that Mr. and Mrs. Baker's house?

B. No. It isn't _____.

4. A. Is this my recipe for meatballs?

B. No. It isn't _____.

D. Fill in the blanks.

Ex. Donald is _____neater than_____ Sam.
                          neat

1. Jane is _____ Sarah.
                tall

2. Carl is _____ Jack.
                honest

3. Centerville is _____ Lakeville.
                      pretty

4. The pie is _____ the cake.
                  good

5. Julie is _____ John.
              dependable

E. Complete the sentences.

Ex. William (rich) _____isn't as_____

_____rich as_____ Walter, but he's

much (happy) _____happier_____.

1. Ann's printer (fast) _____

_____ Betty's printer, but it's much

(reliable) _____.

2. Danny's dog (friendly) _____

_____ Dorothy's dog, but it's much

(cute) _____.

3. Howard (intelligent) _____

_____ Mike, but he's much (interesting)

_____.

4. My apartment (fashionable) _____

_____ your

apartment, but it's much (big)

_____.

5. Tom's furniture (expensive) _____

_____ John's

furniture, but it's much (attractive)

_____.

F. Fill in the blanks.

Ex. Brian is _____the smartest_____ person
                     smart
I know.

1. Marvin is _____ person
                    quiet
I know.

2. Uncle Bert is _____
                        hospitable
person in our family.

3. We have _____
                    large
apartment in the building.

4. Mr. Peterson is _____
                           patient
teacher in our school.

5. Mel is _____ person
                 lazy
I know.

G. Listen and circle the correct answer.

Ex.

| Ronald | Yes / No | Fred |

1. Bob — Yes / No — Bill

2. $6/lb. — Yes / No — $4/lb.

3. Moscow — Yes / No — Miami

4. Herbert — Yes / No — Steven

5. Pam — Yes / No — Patty

Read the article on student book page 59 and answer the questions.

1. The _____ is in New York City.
   a. biggest igloo in the world
   b. longest car in the world
   c. biggest costume party in the world
   d. biggest subway station in the world

2. *Igloos* are _____.
   a. hotels that stay open in winter
   b. buildings made of hard snow
   c. hotels with many rooms
   d. Swedish hotels

3. More than 500,000 people _____.
   a. walk through Grand Central Terminal every day
   b. walk through the streets of Brazil in costume every day during Carnival
   c. stay at the Ice Hotel every year
   d. ride in the world's longest car every day

4. In Brazil people wear _____ to celebrate Carnival.
   a. costume parties
   b. bathing suits
   c. costumes
   d. evening gowns

5. The longest car in the world _____.
   a. has a waterbed to swim in
   b. is twenty-six feet long
   c. is a hundred meters long
   d. has 13 wheels on each side

6. According to this article, the Ice Hotel _____.
   a. has a swimming pool
   b. starts to turn to water when it's warm
   c. always has 150 guests
   d. is popular in the spring

B DO YOU KNOW? Your Country

Answer these questions about your country.

1. What's the largest city? ....

2. What's the longest highway or road? ....

3. What's the most popular vacation place? ....

4. What's the most popular tourist sight? ....

5. What's the most popular food? ....

C DO YOU KNOW? The Longest and Shortest Words

Look in an English dictionary and in a dictionary in your language.

1. What's the longest word you can find in English? ....

2. What does it mean? ....

3. What's the longest word you can find in your language? ....

4. What does it mean? ....

D BUILD YOUR VOCABULARY! Prefixes

Complete the following words with the correct negative prefix.

1. _____polite   5. _____friendly

2. _____safe   6. _____honest

3. _____healthy   7. _____comfortable

4. _____expensive   8. _____patient

E BUILD YOUR VOCABULARY! What's the Word?

Choose the correct word from the answers in Exercise D.

1. I really don't need another shirt, but I'll buy this one because it's _____.

2. That car doesn't have any seat belts. Don't ride in it! It's _____!

3. Alex takes things in a store and doesn't pay for them. He's very _____.

4. There's too much sugar in those donuts. They're very _____.

5. I don't sleep well at night because my bed is _____.

6. Luis wants to learn to speak English right away. He's _____.

7. Don't talk when you have food in your mouth! It's _____.

8. People think Gloria is _____ because she's shy and likes to be alone.

F BUILD YOUR VOCABULARY! Prefix or No Prefix?

Choose the correct word from Exercise D—either with or without a negative prefix.

1. Butter and sugar aren't good for you, but vegetables are _____.

2. Harvey always says thank you, but his brother Howard is very _____.

3. These shoes feel good on my feet, but those shoes are _____.

4. You can never believe anything Clara says, but her sister is very _____.

5. This dress doesn't cost a lot of money, but that dress is very _____.

6. Daniel can wait for hours and never get upset, but his son Steven is very

   _____.

7. George never smiles or says hello, but his brother Robert is very _____.

8. You won't have an accident in this car, but that car is _____.

G BUILD YOUR VOCABULARY! What's the Prefix?

Can you guess the correct prefix? Write *un* or *in* before the adjective to complete these conversations.

1. A. Is your landlord a kind person?

   B. No. My landlord is a very _____ person.

2. A. Do your parents wear fashionable clothing?

   B. No. They wear very _____ clothing.

3. A. Are the buses in your city reliable?

   B. No. They're always late. They're very _____.

4. A. Is your apartment building in a convenient neighborhood?

   B. No. It isn't near any stores or bus stops. It's in a very _____ neighborhood.

5. A. Is that television program about the Pacific Ocean interesting?

   B. No. There isn't much information in the program. It's very _____.

6. A. Are your neighbors hospitable?

   B. Not really. They never invite people to visit them. They're very _____.

H FACT FILE

Look at the Fact File on student book page 59 and answer the questions.

1. The Nile is a long _____.
   a. ocean
   b. desert
   c. mountain
   d. river

2. The largest ocean in the world is sixty-four million _____.
   a. miles long
   b. kilometers long
   c. square miles
   d. square kilometers

3. The Sahara is a large _____.
   a. ocean
   b. desert
   c. mountain
   d. river

4. The longest river in the world is 4,180 _____ long.
   a. feet
   b. miles
   c. meters
   d. kilometers

5. Mount Everest is _____ meters high.
   a. four thousand one hundred eighty
   b. twenty-nine thousand twenty-eight
   c. six thousand six hundred ninety
   d. eight thousand eight hundred forty-eight

6. There are 1000 meters in a kilometer. Mount Everest is almost _____ high.
   a. nine kilometers
   b. eighty-nine kilometers
   c. eight hundred ninety kilometers
   d. eighty-eight kilometers

7. The Nile is six thousand six hundred ninety
_____.
   a. miles long
   b. kilometers long
   c. miles high
   d. square kilometers

8. Sixty-four million square miles _____
165,760,000 square kilometers.
   a. is a little more than
   b. is much more than
   c. isn't as much as
   d. is the same as

9. The Sahara _____ nine million square
kilometers.
   a. is
   b. is less than
   c. is more than
   d. is much less than

10. The Pacific Ocean _____.
   a. is 165,760,000 kilometers long
   b. is larger than the Atlantic Ocean
   c. isn't as large as the Sahara desert
   d. isn't as large as the Atlantic Ocean

"CAN-DO" REVIEW

Match the "can do" statement and the correct sentence.

____ 1. I can make an invitation.

____ 2. I can ask about future plans.

____ 3. I can express certainty.

____ 4. I can express uncertainty.

____ 5. I can warn someone.

____ 6. I can agree with someone.

____ 7. I can disagree with someone.

____ 8. I can make comparisons.

____ 9. I can offer to help a customer.

____ 10. I can apologize to a customer.

a. I'm positive!

b. Careful! Watch your step!

c. Would you like to go to the movies with me?

d. I think so, too.

e. Sorry we can't help you.

f. I really can't decide.

g. May I help you?

h. I disagree with you.

i. What are you going to do this evening?

j. The streets in your town are cleaner than
the streets in our town.

across from	on the right	walk up
between	on the left	walk down
next to		

STUDENT BOOK
PAGES 61–70

SOUTH ST.

barber shop	library
clinic	toy store
shoe store	post office
bakery	book store
bank	drug store
high school	police station

1. **A.** Excuse me. Can you tell me how to get to the library from here?

   B. ___Walk up___ South Street and you'll see

   the library ___on the right___,

   ___across from___ the barber shop.

HIGH SCHOOL

2. **A.** Excuse me. Can you tell me how to get to the clinic from here?

   B. _____ South Street and you'll

   see the clinic _____,

   _____ the shoe store.

POLICE STATION

3. **A.** Excuse me. Can you tell me how to get to the toy store from here?

   B. _____ South Street and you'll

   see the toy store _____,

   _____ the clinic.

BANK

4. **A.** Excuse me. Can you tell me how to get to the drug store from here?

   B. _____ South Street and you'll see the drug store

   _____, _____ the book store and

   the police station.

BARBER SHOP

5. **A.** Excuse me. Can you tell me how to get to the high school from here?

   B. _____ South Street and you'll see the high school

   _____, _____ the bank and

   _____ the police station.

LIBRARY

across from
between
next to
on the left
on the right

walk along
walk down
walk up

| playground | SOUTH STREET | police station | | | | |
| school | | bank | hotel | park | museum |

X ← You are here.   ELM STREET

| post office | | restaurant | zoo | parking lot | university |
| hospital | | bus station |

1. A. Excuse me. Could you please tell me how to get to the university from here?

   B. ____Walk along____ Elm Street and you'll see the university

   ___on the right___ , ___across from___ the museum.

2. A. Excuse me. Could you please tell me how to get to the park from here?

   B. _____ Elm Street and you'll see the park

   _____ , _____ the hotel.

3. A. Excuse me. Could you please tell me how to get to the police station from here?

   B. _____ South Street and you'll see the police station

   _____ , _____ the playground.

4. A. Excuse me. Could you please tell me how to get to the bus station from here?

   B. _____ South Street and you'll see the bus station

   _____ , _____ the restaurant.

5. A. Excuse me. Could you please tell me how to get to the zoo from here?

   B. _____ Elm Street and you'll see the zoo

   _____ , _____ the restaurant and
   the parking lot.

| gas station | fire station | | flower shop | cafeteria | post office | | motel | clinic |

EIGHTH AVENUE

park	courthouse		shoe store	pet shop	library		hospital	restaurant
	ice cream shop	ELM STREET	playground	museum		OAK STREET	toy store
department store	book store		hardware store	parking garage			concert hall

NINTH AVENUE

| zoo | supermarket | | shopping mall | hotel | | bus station |

Mr. and Mrs. Lee are very busy today. They want to go several places with their children, but they don't know the city very well. They need your help.

1. They're at the shopping mall, and they want to take their children to the toy store to buy them a new toy. Tell them how to get there.

___Walk along___ Ninth Avenue to Oak Street and

___turn left___. ___Walk up___ Oak Street

and you'll see the toy store ___on the right___,

___across from___ the museum.

2. They're at the toy store, and now they want to take their children to the pet shop to buy them a dog.

_____ Oak Street to Eighth Avenue and

_____. _____ Eighth

Avenue and you'll see the pet shop _____,

_____ the shoe store and the library.

3. They're at the pet shop, and they want to take their children to the ice cream shop for some ice cream.

4. They're at the ice cream shop, and they want to take their children to the zoo.

5. They're at the zoo, and they're tired. They want to go to the park to rest.

6. They had a wonderful day, and now it's time to go home. Tell them how to get to the bus station.

_____ Eighth Avenue to Elm Street and

_____. _____ Elm Street

and you'll see the ice cream shop _____,

_____ the courthouse.

_____ Elm Street to Ninth Avenue and

_____. _____ Ninth

Avenue and you'll see the zoo _____,

_____ the department store.

....

....

....

....

....

....

....

....

D LISTENING 🔊

Look at the map on page 62. Listen and choose the correct answer.

1. (a.) She was hungry.
    b.   She wanted to buy a bird.

2. a.   He wanted to look at paintings.
    b.   He wanted to listen to music.

3. a.   They wanted to read some books.
    b.   They wanted to buy some flowers.

4. a.   She wanted to buy some toys for her son.
    b.   She wanted to visit her sick friend.

5. a.   He wanted to buy some groceries.
    b.   He wanted to look at the animals.

6. a.   She was sick.
    b.   She was hungry.

Listen. Then clap and practice.

A. I have a terrible · sense of · direction.

I never know · which way to · go!

All. This way or · that way?

This way or · that way?

A. I never know · which way to · go!

I think that it's · that way, but · maybe I'm · wrong.

I never know · which way to · go!

B. I have a wonderful · sense of · direction.

I always know · which way to · go!

All. Turn · left!

Turn · right!

B. I always know · which way to · go!

I know that it's · that way.

I'm never · wrong!

I always know · which way to · go!

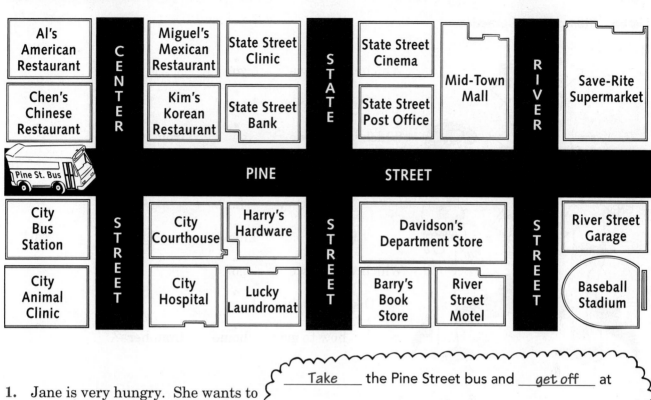

1. Jane is very hungry. She wants to have Mexican food for dinner. Tell her the best way to get to Miguel's Mexican Restaurant.

__Take__ the Pine Street bus and __get off__ at __Center Street__. __Walk up__ __Center__ Street and you'll see Miguel's Mexican Restaurant __on the right__.

2. Ricky and his friends are late for the baseball game. Tell them the fastest way to get to the baseball stadium.

_____ the Pine Street bus and _____ at _____. _____ _____ Street and you'll see the baseball stadium _____.

3. Amanda and her mother are late for a movie. Tell them how to get to the State Street Cinema.

_____ the Pine Street bus and _____ at _____. _____ _____ Street and you'll see the State Street Cinema _____.

4. Tony's dog is sick. Tell him the shortest way to get to the City Animal Clinic.

....
....
....

G **GRAMMARRAP:** *Which Way Do We Go?*

Listen. Then clap and practice.

Which way do we   go?

Does anybody   know?

Which way do we   go   from here?

Is it very   near?

Is it very   far?

I wish I   knew   where I left my   car!

Which way do we   go?

Does anybody   know

how to get   home   from here?

H **GRAMMARRAP:** *Turn Right!*

Listen. Then clap and practice.

A.   Turn   right   at the next   light.

B.   At the next   light?

A.   That's right.

A.   Don't   turn left!   Turn right!

B.   At the light?

A.   That's right.   Turn right   at the light.

A.   Make a left   at the next   light.

B.   Make a left?

A.   That's right,   make a left   at the light.

Make a left   at the light   and then   turn right.

Make a left   at the next   light.

66   **Activity Workbook**

I LISTENING: *Where Did They Go?*

```
                        DAY STREET
Day St. Bus

┌─────────────────────┐ F ┌─────────────────────┐ S ┌─────────────────────┐ T
│   shopping mall     │ I │      museum         │ E │      hospital       │ H
│                     │ R │                     │ C │                     │ I
├───────┬──────┬──────┤ S ├──────┬──────┬───────┤ O ├──────┬──────┬───────┤ R
│bakery │ bus  │hotel │ T │ ice  │motel │clinic │ N │high  │post  │ park  │ D
│       │station│     │   │cream │      │       │ D │school│office│       │
│       │      │      │   │ shop │      │       │   │      │      │       │ S
                        T                         S                       T
                    BRIGHTON BOULEVARD                                    R
┌───────┬──────┬──────┐ S ┌──────┬──────┬───────┐ S ┌──────┬──────┬───────┐ E
│barber │book  │drug  │ T │parking│toy  │ gas   │ T │police│ bank │ pet   │ E
│ shop  │store │store │ R │ lot  │store │station│ R │station│     │ shop  │ T
├───────┴──────┼──────┤ E ├──────┼──────┼───────┤ E ├──────┼──────┼───────┤
│concert hall  │ zoo  │ E │flower│library│church│ E │shoe  │parking│fire  │
│              │      │ T │ shop │      │       │ T │store │garage│station│
Bay Ave. Bus
                        BAY AVENUE
```

Listen and fill in the correct places.

1. He went to the _____bank_____.

2. She went to the _____.

3. They went to the _____.

4. She went to the _____.

5. They went to the _____.

6. He went to the _____.

J WHAT'S THE WORD?

between	could	from	how	off	subway	turn	walk
certainly	excuse	get	left	please	take	up	

A. ___Excuse___¹ me. _____² you _____³

tell me _____⁴ to _____⁵ to the train

station _____⁶ here?

B. _____⁷. _____⁸ the

_____⁹ and get _____¹⁰ at Park Street.

Walk _____¹¹ Park Street to Tenth Avenue

and _____¹² right. _____¹³ along Tenth

Avenue and you'll see the train station on the

_____¹⁴, _____¹⁵ the post office
and the fire station.

Activity Workbook   67

CHECK-UP TESTS
SKILLS CHECKS

Choose the correct answer.

1. Brian is very athletic. He likes to ____.
   - Ⓐ chat online
   - Ⓑ watch videos
   - Ⓒ go hiking
   - Ⓓ cook

2. I ____ my home and bought a condominium.
   - Ⓐ sent
   - Ⓑ gave
   - Ⓒ moved
   - Ⓓ sold

3. I live on the West Coast, and you live on the East Coast. We live ____ each other.
   - Ⓐ near
   - Ⓑ far apart from
   - Ⓒ between
   - Ⓓ next to

4. I ____ with my friends over the Internet.
   - Ⓐ call
   - Ⓑ grow up
   - Ⓒ send
   - Ⓓ communicate

5. When I have a problem, my parents always give me good ____.
   - Ⓐ advice
   - Ⓑ message
   - Ⓒ friends
   - Ⓓ letters

6. ____ today. ____ every day.
   - Ⓐ He's watching TV . . . He watches TV
   - Ⓑ He's cooking . . . He's cooking
   - Ⓒ We read . . . We're reading
   - Ⓓ She studies . . . She studies

7. ____ on your day off?
   - Ⓐ What like you to do
   - Ⓑ Do you like to do
   - Ⓒ What you like to do
   - Ⓓ What do you like to do

8. They ____ downtown last weekend. They ____ downtown very often.
   - Ⓐ drove . . . don't like drive
   - Ⓑ like to drive . . . don't drive
   - Ⓒ drove . . . don't like to drive
   - Ⓓ didn't drive . . . don't like to drove

9. What ____ for their anniversary?
   - Ⓐ did you give them
   - Ⓑ are you going to them give
   - Ⓒ did you gave them
   - Ⓓ you give them

10. He ____ his wife a blouse for her birthday. He ____ a blouse last year.
    - Ⓐ can buy her . . . didn't buy her
    - Ⓑ can't buy . . . bought her
    - Ⓒ bought . . . bought her his wife
    - Ⓓ buys . . . bought his wife her

SKILLS CHECK

Match the "can do" statement and the correct sentence.

____ 1. I can say the days of the week.

____ 2. I can say the months of the year.

____ 3. I can name the seasons.

____ 4. I can tell about favorite activities.

____ 5. I can ask about favorite activities.

____ 6. I can ask about future plans.

____ 7. I can ask about past activities.

____ 8. I can tell about dislikes.

a. What did you do yesterday?

b. I like to swim.

c. What are you going to do tomorrow?

d. Spring, summer, winter, fall.

e. I don't like to dance.

f. January, February, March, . . .

g. What do you like to do on the weekend?

h. Sunday, Monday, Tuesday, . . .

Choose the correct answer.

1. Do you want to bake some _____ today?
   - Ⓐ salad
   - Ⓑ ice cream
   - Ⓒ cookies
   - Ⓓ coffee

2. When I'm thirsty, I usually like to drink _____.
   - Ⓐ milk
   - Ⓑ lettuce
   - Ⓒ mayonnaise
   - Ⓓ lemons

3. Aunt Clara's _____ always tastes delicious.
   - Ⓐ kitchen
   - Ⓑ chicken
   - Ⓒ cabinet
   - Ⓓ counter

4. My favorite dessert is _____.
   - Ⓐ cake
   - Ⓑ ketchup
   - Ⓒ mustard
   - Ⓓ pepper

5. Mr. and Mrs. Mendoza _____ seventy-five dollars at the supermarket.
   - Ⓐ lent
   - Ⓑ bought
   - Ⓒ spent
   - Ⓓ sold

6. The mayonnaise _____ in the refrigerator and the soy sauce _____ in the cabinet.
   - Ⓐ are . . . are
   - Ⓑ is . . . are
   - Ⓒ are . . . is
   - Ⓓ is . . . is

7. I made tonight's dinner. I'm glad _____.
   - Ⓐ you liked them
   - Ⓑ you liked it
   - Ⓒ they liked you
   - Ⓓ it liked you

8. A. _____ juice do you want?
   B. Just _____.
   - Ⓐ How many . . . not too many
   - Ⓑ How much . . . not much
   - Ⓒ How many . . . a few
   - Ⓓ How much . . . a little

9. We can't make a salad for lunch because _____ lettuce and _____ tomatoes.
   - Ⓐ there aren't any . . . there aren't any
   - Ⓑ there isn't any . . . there isn't any
   - Ⓒ there isn't any . . . there aren't any
   - Ⓓ it isn't any . . . they aren't any

10. I can't believe I spent so much money! I just bought _____, and I didn't buy _____.
    - Ⓐ a few lemons . . . very much flour
    - Ⓑ a few rice . . . very many onions
    - Ⓒ a little carrots . . . very much cheese
    - Ⓓ a little tea . . . very many mayonnaise

SKILLS CHECK

Match the "can do" statement and the correct sentence.

_____ 1. I can ask the location of food items.

_____ 2. I can make a suggestion.

_____ 3. I can offer food.

_____ 4. I can compliment about food.

_____ 5. I can tell about food I like.

_____ 6. I can tell about food I dislike.

_____ 7. I can tell about food purchases.

a. This chicken is delicious!

b. I think vegetables are delicious.

c. Where's the ice cream?

d. I bought a few oranges.

e. Let's make pizza for lunch!

f. I think yogurt tastes terrible.

g. Would you care for some more cake?

Choose the correct answer.

1. I ordered a _____ for dessert.
   - Ⓐ bowl of soup
   - Ⓑ bag of flour
   - Ⓒ piece of pie
   - Ⓓ loaf of bread

2. I'm slicing some _____.
   - Ⓐ tomatoes
   - Ⓑ sugar
   - Ⓒ soup
   - Ⓓ juice

3. I recommend our _____ for breakfast.
   - Ⓐ flour
   - Ⓑ chocolate ice cream
   - Ⓒ lettuce
   - Ⓓ pancakes

4. Next, chop up some _____.
   - Ⓐ jam
   - Ⓑ nuts
   - Ⓒ flour
   - Ⓓ milk

5. The recipe says to pour in some _____.
   - Ⓐ fish
   - Ⓑ bread
   - Ⓒ cheese
   - Ⓓ water

6. Cheese _____ expensive this week, but lettuce _____ very cheap.
   - Ⓐ are . . . is
   - Ⓑ is . . . is
   - Ⓒ is . . . are
   - Ⓓ are . . . are

7. We need a _____ milk and a _____ eggs.
   - Ⓐ quart . . . pound
   - Ⓑ pint of . . . bunch of
   - Ⓒ half gallon of . . . dozen of
   - Ⓓ quart of . . . dozen

8. I looked in the refrigerator and _____ any carrots and _____ any orange juice.
   - Ⓐ weren't . . . wasn't
   - Ⓑ there wasn't . . . weren't
   - Ⓒ there weren't . . . there wasn't
   - Ⓓ there wasn't . . . there wasn't

9. Please give me _____ french fries. Everybody says _____ fantastic.
   - Ⓐ order . . . they're
   - Ⓑ an order of . . . their
   - Ⓒ an order of . . . they're
   - Ⓓ order of . . . it's

10. You need to add _____ butter and _____ raisins.
    - Ⓐ a little more . . . a few more
    - Ⓑ little . . . few more
    - Ⓒ more a little . . . more a few
    - Ⓓ a little more . . . few more

SKILLS CHECK ✓

Match the "can do" statement and the correct sentence.

_____ 1. I can express food needs to make a shopping list.

_____ 2. I can ask about food prices.

_____ 3. I can agree with someone.

_____ 4. I can get someone's attention.

_____ 5. I can ask the location of food in the supermarket.

_____ 6. I can ask for a recommendation.

_____ 7. I can make a recommendation.

_____ 8. I can give recipe instructions.

a. What do you recommend?

b. You're right.

c. I'm looking for carrots.

d. We need a loaf of bread.

e. Put a little butter into a saucepan.

f. I suggest the pancakes.

g. How much does a head of lettuce cost?

h. Excuse me.

Choose the correct answer.

1. The _____ will arrive in fifteen minutes.
   - Ⓐ game
   - Ⓑ train
   - Ⓒ vacation
   - Ⓓ measles

2. My husband and I are going on vacation. We'll be back _____.
   - Ⓐ in a few minutes
   - Ⓑ this afternoon
   - Ⓒ in half an hour
   - Ⓓ in a week

3. Fred! Don't touch that wire! You might _____.
   - Ⓐ get a shock
   - Ⓑ see your doctor
   - Ⓒ get seasick
   - Ⓓ drown

4. I'm going to call a doctor. I think my son might _____.
   - Ⓐ bloom
   - Ⓑ be sick and tired of the weather
   - Ⓒ have the flu
   - Ⓓ be famous

5. Careful! Watch your step! You might _____.
   - Ⓐ fall asleep
   - Ⓑ fall
   - Ⓒ catch a cold
   - Ⓓ get sick

6. A. Do you think there will be many people at the party?
   B. Maybe _____ and maybe _____.
   - Ⓐ they will . . . they won't
   - Ⓑ there are . . . they aren't
   - Ⓒ there will . . . there won't
   - Ⓓ there will . . . they won't

7. Ms. Martinez will be back _____ an hour.
   - Ⓐ in
   - Ⓑ at
   - Ⓒ on
   - Ⓓ in a half

8. _____ be spring soon. The weather _____ nice.
   - Ⓐ We'll . . . will
   - Ⓑ Will . . . it'll be
   - Ⓒ It'll will . . . will be
   - Ⓓ It'll . . . will be

9. I don't want to go skiing with you. I'm afraid _____ break my leg.
   - Ⓐ I'll might
   - Ⓑ I might
   - Ⓒ might I
   - Ⓓ I might will

10. Tom is sick. He _____ go to work today, and he also _____ go to work tomorrow.
    - Ⓐ won't . . . might
    - Ⓑ will . . . might not to
    - Ⓒ won't . . . might not
    - Ⓓ might . . . won't not

SKILLS CHECK ✓

Match the "can do" statement and the correct sentence.

_____ 1. I can ask when a future event will occur.

_____ 2. I can ask about future plans.

_____ 3. I can express uncertainty.

_____ 4. I can warn someone.

_____ 5. I can ask for repetition.

_____ 6. I can make an invitation.

_____ 7. I can express fear.

_____ 8. I can express certainty.

a. I really can't decide.

b. I'm sorry. What did you say?

c. Will the train arrive soon?

d. I'm positive!

e. I'm afraid I might get sick.

f. Careful! Put on your helmet!

g. What are you going to do tonight?

h. Would you like to go dancing with me?

Choose the correct answer.

1. I think our new living room furniture is very _____.
   Ⓐ intelligent
   Ⓑ comfortable
   Ⓒ honest
   Ⓓ friendly

2. It's important to eat _____ food.
   Ⓐ bad
   Ⓑ sympathetic
   Ⓒ large
   Ⓓ healthy

3. Everybody says the subway system in our city is very _____.
   Ⓐ polite
   Ⓑ talkative
   Ⓒ reliable
   Ⓓ understanding

4. You shouldn't buy that coat. It isn't very _____.
   Ⓐ attractive
   Ⓑ spicy
   Ⓒ short
   Ⓓ neat

5. I think we should hire Ramon. He'll be a _____ secretary.
   Ⓐ lazy
   Ⓑ capable
   Ⓒ light
   Ⓓ wide

6. My new boss _____ my old boss.
   Ⓐ is nicer than
   Ⓑ is nicer
   Ⓒ isn't as nice
   Ⓓ is more nice than

7. You shouldn't buy a fan. An air conditioner is _____ a fan.
   Ⓐ convenient than
   Ⓑ powerfuller than
   Ⓒ more powerful than
   Ⓓ louder as

8. I think _____ plant flowers. They're _____ vegetables.
   Ⓐ you should . . . more pretty than
   Ⓑ you shouldn't . . . prettier as
   Ⓒ you shouldn't . . . useful than
   Ⓓ you should . . . prettier than

9. A. My car isn't _____ Henry's car.
   B. Don't be ridiculous! Yours is _____ his.
   Ⓐ fast as . . . fast as
   Ⓑ as fast as . . . much faster than
   Ⓒ as fast as . . . much more fast than
   Ⓓ as faster as . . . much faster than

10. A. In my opinion, my street _____ yours.
    B. I disagree. Your street is _____ mine.
    Ⓐ isn't as nice as . . . much nicer than
    Ⓑ is safer as . . . more safe than
    Ⓒ isn't as wide as . . . as wider than
    Ⓓ is busier than . . . more busier than

SKILLS CHECK

Match the "can do" statement and the correct sentence.

_____ 1. I can make comparisons.

_____ 2. I can agree with someone.

_____ 3. I can ask for advice.

_____ 4. I can give advice.

_____ 5. I can disagree with someone.

_____ 6. I can express certainty.

_____ 7. I can express an opinion.

a. That's right.

b. In my opinion, the streets in our city are safe.

c. I don't think so.

d. I think you should buy a bicycle.

e. The weather in Miami is better than the weather in New York.

f. Should I buy a used car or a new car?

g. Definitely!

Choose the correct answer.

1. The new mall is in a _____ location.
   - Ⓐ short
   - Ⓑ convenient
   - Ⓒ lightweight
   - Ⓓ stubborn

2. George is a wonderful salesperson. He's always _____.
   - Ⓐ helpful
   - Ⓑ noisy
   - Ⓒ rude
   - Ⓓ sloppy

3. Everybody compliments us about our son. They say he's the _____ boy in the neighborhood.
   - Ⓐ worst
   - Ⓑ laziest
   - Ⓒ friendliest
   - Ⓓ most boring

4. This is the most _____ stove we have.
   - Ⓐ patient
   - Ⓑ generous
   - Ⓒ honest
   - Ⓓ dependable

5. Nobody likes the man in Apartment 5. He's very _____.
   - Ⓐ bright
   - Ⓑ nice
   - Ⓒ mean
   - Ⓓ kind

6. Robert is _____ person I know.
   - Ⓐ friendliest
   - Ⓑ most friendly
   - Ⓒ the most friendliest
   - Ⓓ the friendliest

7. Everybody agrees that Aunt Margaret is _____ person in our family.
   - Ⓐ the honestest
   - Ⓑ the most honest
   - Ⓒ most honest
   - Ⓓ the most honestest

8. Ricardo is _____ and _____ student in our class.
   - Ⓐ smartest . . . most talented
   - Ⓑ the most smart . . . the most talent
   - Ⓒ the smartest . . . the most talented
   - Ⓓ the most smartest . . . the talentest

9. This store isn't _____ even though it's _____.
   - Ⓐ the most popular . . . the best
   - Ⓑ the popularist . . . the nicest
   - Ⓒ the most popular . . . the most cheap
   - Ⓓ most popular . . . most convenient

10. I'm sorry. We don't have _____ printer. This is _____ in the store.
    - Ⓐ a smallest . . . the smallest
    - Ⓑ the smaller . . . smallest
    - Ⓒ a smaller . . . the most smallest
    - Ⓓ a smaller . . . the smallest

SKILLS CHECK

Match the "can do" statement and the correct sentence.

_____ 1. I can describe people.

_____ 2. I can agree with someone.

_____ 3. I can express an opinion.

_____ 4. I can offer to help a customer.

_____ 5. I can ask for an item in a store.

_____ 6. I can apologize to a customer.

_____ 7. I can describe things.

a. Sorry we can't help you.

b. If you ask me, . . .

c. I want to buy a cheap watch.

d. It's very small.

e. Your parents are very nice.

f. May I help you?

g. I agree.

Choose the correct answer.

1. I go to the _____ on Main Street to wash my shirts.
   (A) shopping mall
   (B) department store
   (C) hardware store
   (D) laundromat

2. They bake wonderful pies and cakes at the _____ down the street.
   (A) bank
   (B) bakery
   (C) barber shop
   (D) flower shop

3. I got off the bus at the wrong _____.
   (A) stop
   (B) map
   (C) bus
   (D) directions

4. We don't want to be late for the plane. What's the fastest way to get to the _____?
   (A) train station
   (B) bus station
   (C) airport
   (D) gas station

5. Can you _____ a good department store?
   (A) tell me how
   (B) directions
   (C) how to get there
   (D) recommend

6. Walk _____ Main Street _____ Washington Boulevard.
   (A) up . . . to
   (B) down . . . for
   (C) along . . . at
   (D) from . . . between

7. Walk down Central Avenue to Riverside Road and _____.
   (A) right turn
   (B) turn left
   (C) walk left
   (D) turn at the left

8. _____ the subway and _____ Grand Avenue.
   (A) Turn on . . . get up at
   (B) Take . . . go off for
   (C) Make . . . get off to
   (D) Take . . . get off at

9. _____ the football stadium _____.
   (A) You'll see . . . on the right
   (B) Take . . . at the left
   (C) You'll know . . . across from the zoo
   (D) Turn . . . at the right

10. Walk up Broadway one block _____ the corner _____ Elm Street and Pine.
    (A) on . . . for
    (B) at . . . in
    (C) to . . . of
    (D) of . . . on

SKILLS CHECK

Match the "can do" statement and the correct sentence.

_____ 1. I can ask for directions to a place.

_____ 2. I can give directions to a place.

_____ 3. I can get someone's attention.

_____ 4. I can express gratitude.

_____ 5. I can ask for repetition.

_____ 6. I can ask for a recommendation.

_____ 7. I can give a recommendation.

a. Can you recommend a good restaurant?

b. Thanks very much.

c. Could you please say that again?

d. Walk up Main Street and you'll see the clinic on the right.

e. I think it's one of the best restaurants in town.

f. Can you tell me how to get to the post office?

g. Excuse me.

APPENDIX

Student Book Listening Scripts

Chapter 1 – Page 9

Listen and choose the correct answer.

1. What are you going to do tomorrow?
2. What do you do in the summer?
3. When did you clean your apartment?
4. What did you give your parents for their anniversary?
5. Where did you and your friends go yesterday?
6. How often do they send messages to each other?
7. What did he give her?
8. When are you going to make pancakes?

Chapter 2 – Page 16

Listen and choose what the people are talking about.

1. A. How much do you want?
   B. Just a little, please.
2. A. Do you want some more?
   B. Okay. But just a few.
3. A. These are delicious!
   B. I'm glad you like them.
4. A. I ate too many.
   B. How many did you eat?
5. A. They're bad for my health.
   B. Really?
6. A. It's very good.
   B. Thank you.
7. A. Would you care for some more?
   B. Yes, but not too much.
8. A. There isn't any.
   B. There isn't?!

Chapter 3 – Page 22

Listen and choose what the people are talking about.

1. A. How much does a gallon cost?
   B. Two seventy-nine.
2. A. They're very expensive this week.
   B. You're right.
3. A. How many loaves do we need?
   B. Three.
4. A. Sorry. There aren't any more.
   B. There aren't?!
5. A. I need two pounds.
   B. Two pounds? Okay.
6. A. How much does the large box cost?
   B. Five thirty-nine.
7. A. How many cans do we need?
   B. Three.
8. A. I bought too much.
   B. Really?

Side by Side Gazette – Page 28

Listen and match the products and the prices.

1. Attention, food shoppers! Thank you for shopping at Save-Rite Supermarket! Crispy Cereal is on sale this week. A box of Crispy Cereal is only three dollars and forty-nine cents. Three forty-nine is a very good price for Crispy Cereal. So buy some today!
2. Attention, shoppers! Right now in the bakery section whole wheat bread is on sale. Buy a loaf of whole wheat bread for only two seventy-five. That's right! Just two seventy-five! The bread is hot and fresh. So come to the bakery section and get a loaf now!
3. Thank you for shopping at Sunny Supermarket! We have a special low price on orange juice today. A quart of orange juice is only a dollar seventy-nine. Orange juice is in Aisle 5, next to the milk.
4. Hello, food shoppers! It's 95 degrees today. It's a good day for Sorelli's ice cream! Sorelli's ice cream comes in vanilla, chocolate, and other delicious flavors. And today, a pint of Sorelli's ice cream is only three twenty-five!
5. Welcome to Bartley's Supermarket! We have a special today on bananas. You can buy bananas for only forty cents a pound. Bananas are good for you! So walk over to our fruit section and buy a bunch of bananas today!

Chapter 4 – Page 37

WHAT'S THE LINE?

Mrs. Harris (from the story on page 36) is calling Tommy and Julie's school. Listen and choose the correct lines.

1. Good morning. Park Elementary School.
2. Yes, Mrs. Harris. What can I do for you?
3. Oh? What's the matter?
4. That's too bad. Are you going to take them to the doctor?
5. Well, I hope Tommy and Julie feel better soon.

WHAT'S THE WORD?

Listen and choose the word you hear.

1. I might go to school tomorrow.
2. I want to come to work today.
3. Don't walk there!
4. We'll be ready in half an hour.
5. They'll go to school tomorrow.
6. Don't stand there! You might get hit!
7. I call the doctor when I'm sick.
8. Watch your step! There are wet spots on the floor.
9. I'm sick and tired of sailing.

Chapter 5 – Page 44

Listen and choose what the people are talking about.

1. A. I like it. It's fast.
   B. It is. It's much faster than my old one.
2. A. Is it comfortable?
   B. Yes. It's more comfortable than my old one.
3. A. I think it should be shorter.
   B. But it's very short now!
4. A. They aren't very polite.
   B. You're right. They should be more polite.
5. A. Is it safe?
   B. Yes. It's much safer than my old one.
6. A. Which one should I buy?
   B. Buy this one. It's more powerful than that one.

Chapter 6 – Page 53

Listen to the sentence. Is the person saying something good or something bad about someone else?

1. She's the nicest person I know.
2. He's the laziest student in our class.
3. He's the most boring person I know.
4. She's the most generous person in our family.
5. They're the most honest people I know.
6. He's the rudest person in our apartment building.
7. He's the most dependable person in our office.
8. She's the kindest neighbor on our street.
9. She's the most stubborn person I know.

Side by Side Gazette – Page 60

Listen and match the products.

ANNOUNCER: Are you looking for a special gift for a special person in your life? A birthday gift? An anniversary present? Come to Rings & Things—the best store in town for rings, necklaces, earrings, bracelets, and other fine things. Rings & Things—on Main Street downtown, or at the East Side Mall.

FRIEND 1: That was an excellent dinner!
FRIEND 2: Thank you. I'm glad you liked it.
FRIEND 1: Can I help you wash the dishes?
FRIEND 2: Thanks. But they're already in the dishwasher.
FRIEND 1: Is your dishwasher on?
FRIEND 2: Yes, it is.
FRIEND 1: I can't believe it! Your dishwasher is MUCH quieter than mine.
FRIEND 2: It's new. We got it at the Big Value Store. They sell the quietest dishwashers in town.
ANNOUNCER: That's right. The Big Value Store sells the quietest dishwashers in town. We also have the largest refrigerators, the most powerful washing machines, and the best ovens. And we also have the best prices! So come to the Big Value Store, on Airport Road, open seven days a week.

PERSON WHO CAN'T FALL ASLEEP: Oh, I can't believe it! It's three o'clock in the morning, and I can't fall asleep. This bed is so uncomfortable! I need a new bed. I need a new bed NOW!
ANNOUNCER: Do you have this problem? Is your bed uncomfortable? Come to Comfort Kingdom for the most comfortable beds you can buy. We also have the most beautiful sofas and the most attractive tables and chairs in the city. And our salespeople are the friendliest and the most helpful in town. So visit Comfort Kingdom today because life is short, and you should be comfortable!

ANNOUNCER: I'm standing here today in front of Electric City so we can talk to a typical customer. Here's a typical customer now. He's leaving the store with a large box. Let's ask him a question. Excuse me, sir. May I ask you a question?
CUSTOMER: Certainly.
ANNOUNCER: What did you buy today?
CUSTOMER: A VCR.
ANNOUNCER: And why did you buy it at Electric City?
CUSTOMER: Because Electric City has the cheapest and the most dependable products in town.
ANNOUNCER: Is this your first time at Electric City?
CUSTOMER: Oh, no! Last year I bought a radio here, and the year before I bought a TV.
ANNOUNCER: And are you happy with those products?
CUSTOMER: Absolutely! The radio is much better than my old one, and the picture on my TV is much bigger and brighter.
ANNOUNCER: So are you a happy customer?
CUSTOMER: Definitely! There's no place like Electric City. It's the best store in town.
ANNOUNCER: Well, there you have it! Another happy Electric City customer. Visit an Electric City store near YOU today!

ANNOUNCER: This is it! It's the biggest sale of the year, and it's this weekend at Recreation Station! That's right. Everything is on sale—sneakers, tennis rackets, footballs, basketballs—everything in the store! It's all on sale at Recreation Station. We're the largest! We're the most convenient! We're the best! And this weekend we're the cheapest! It's the biggest sale of the year, and it's this weekend—only at Recreation Station!

WHAT'S THE WORD?

Listen and choose the word you hear.

1. The clinic is on the right, next to the post office.
2. The library is on the left, across from the park.
3. Walk up Town Road to Main Street.
4. Drive along Fourth Avenue to Station Street.
5. Take the subway to Pond Road.
6. The bus stop is at the corner of Central Avenue and Fifth.
7. Take this bus and get off at Bond Street.

WHERE ARE THEY?

Where are these people? Listen and choose the correct place.

1. A. Do you want to buy this shirt?
   B. Yes, please.
2. A. Please give me an order of chicken.
   B. An order of chicken? Certainly.
3. A. Shh! Please be quiet! People are reading.
   B. Sorry.
4. A. Can I visit my wife?
   B. Yes. She and the baby are in Room 407.
5. A. How much does one head cost?
   B. A dollar fifty-nine.
6. A. Hmm. Where's our car?
   B. I think it's on the third floor.

Activity Workbook Listening Scripts

Page 2 Exercise B

Listen and choose the correct response.

1. What do your friends like to do on the weekend?
2. What does your sister like to do on the weekend?
3. What does your brother like to do on the weekend?
4. What do you and your friends like to do on the weekend?
5. What does your son like to do on the weekend?
6. What do you like to do on the weekend?
7. What does your next-door neighbor like to do on the weekend?
8. What does your cousin Sue like to do on the weekend?

Page 10 Exercise N

Listen and write the ordinal number you hear.

Many people live and work in this large apartment building in New York City.

1. There's a barber shop on the second floor.
2. The Wong family lives on the twelfth floor.
3. The Acme Internet Company is on the thirtieth floor.
4. Bob Richards lives on the thirteenth floor.
5. There's a bank on the third floor.
6. There's a dentist's office on the ninth floor.
7. There's a flower shop on the first floor.
8. The Martinez family lives on the nineteenth floor.
9. Louise Lane works on the seventeenth floor.
10. There's a computer store on the fourth floor.
11. There's an expensive French restaurant on the forty-eighth floor.
12. My apartment is on the fifth floor.
13. The Park family lives on the thirty-fourth floor.
14. Dr. Jacobson has an office on the twenty-sixth floor.
15. The Walker family lives on the sixty-second floor.
16. There's a health club on the eighteenth floor.

Page 13 Exercise C

Listen and choose the correct response.

1. Where's the tea?
2. Where are the oranges?
3. Where's the fish?
4. Where are the cookies?
5. Where's the cake?
6. Where's the rice?
7. Where are the pears?
8. Where's the cheese?

Page 15 Exercise F

Listen and put a check under the correct picture.

1. Let's have some pizza!
2. Where are the eggs?
3. Let's make some fresh orange juice!
4. Let's bake a pie!
5. Where are the potatoes?
6. Let's have a sandwich for lunch!

Page 19 Exercise L

Listen and put a check under the correct picture.

1. A. Would you care for some more?
   B. Yes, please. But not too much.
2. A. Do you like them?
   B. Yes, but my doctor says that too many are bad for my health.
3. A. These are wonderful!
   B. I'm glad you like them. I bought them this morning.
4. A. How much did you eat?
   B. I ate too much!
5. A. I bought it this morning, and it's very good. Would you like a little?
   B. Yes, please.
6. A. I really don't like them.
   B. But they're good for you!
7. A. How do you like them?
   B. They're wonderful.
8. A. Would you care for some more?
   B. Yes, please. But not too much.
9. A. Hmm. This is delicious. Would you care for some more?
   B. Yes, please. But just a little.
10. A. This is delicious!
    B. I'm glad you like it. I made it this morning.

Page 22 Exercise C

Listen to the conversations. Put a check under the foods you hear.

1. A. Do we need anything from the supermarket?
   B. Yes. We need a pound of apples, a bunch of bananas, and a head of lettuce.
2. A. What do we need at the supermarket?
   B. We need a pound of cheese, a box of rice, and a bottle of soda.
3. A. Do we need anything from the supermarket?
   B. Yes. We need a loaf of bread, a pound of onions, and a dozen oranges.
4. A. What do we need at the supermarket?
   B. We need a pound of potatoes, a pint of ice cream, and a jar of mustard.

Page 24 Exercise F

Listen and circle the price you hear.

1. A box of cereal costs a dollar ninety-nine.
2. Two cans cost five dollars.
3. Three jars cost four dollars and seventy-nine cents.
4. It costs twenty-five cents.
5. A bottle costs two forty-seven.
6. Two boxes cost six dollars and sixty cents.
7. Three thirteen?! That's a lot of money!
8. A pound costs a dollar fifty.
9. Two dollars and ten cents?! That's cheap!

Page 27 Exercise M

Listen and choose the correct word to complete the sentence.

1. Add a little . . .
2. Chop up a few . . .
3. Cut up a few . . .
4. Pour in a little . . .
5. Slice a few . . .
6. Mix in a little . . .

Page 29 Exercise E

Listen and circle the correct word.

Ex. I want some lemons.
1. I'd like some ice cream.
2. I need some tomatoes.
3. I'm looking for lettuce.
4. May I have some meatballs?
5. I want some whole wheat bread.

Page 32 Exercise D

Listen and circle the words you hear.

1. I want to have the chocolate ice cream.
2. They won't fax the letter this morning.
3. I want to recommend the fish today.
4. Peter and William won't go home this morning.
5. She won't eat meat.
6. They want to get married soon.
7. He won't buy a car this year.
8. We want to use our computer now.

Page 37 Exercise K

Listen and choose the correct answer.

1. I'm afraid I might get sick!
2. I'm afraid I might fall asleep!
3. I'm afraid I might step on your feet!
4. I'm afraid I might break my leg!
5. I'm afraid I might catch a cold!
6. I'm afraid I might drown.
7. I'm afraid I might get seasick!
8. I'm afraid I might get a sunburn!
9. I'm afraid I might have a terrible time!
10. I'm afraid I might look terrible!

Page 42 Exercise F

Listen and choose the correct words to complete the sentences.

1. A. Yesterday was cool.
   B. I know. But today is . . .
2. A. Ronald is tall.
   B. You're right. But his son Jim is . . .
3. A. This briefcase is very attractive.
   B. Really? I think THAT briefcase is . . .
4. A. Nancy is very nice.
   B. Do you know her sister Sally? She's . . .
5. A. Tom is very fast.
   B. You're right. But his brother John is . . .
6. A. Michael is a very friendly person.
   B. I know. But his wife is . . .
7. A. Your roommate is very interesting.
   B. You're right. But I think YOUR roommate is . . .
8. A. The supermarket on Center Street was very busy today.
   B. Yes, I know. But the supermarket on Main Street was . . .

Page 44 Exercise I

Listen and circle the correct answer.

1. Yesterday was hotter than today.
2. The tomatoes are more expensive than the potatoes.
3. Aunt Betty is younger than cousin Jane.
4. Bob is shorter and heavier than Bill.
5. Barry's chair is more comfortable than Larry's chair.
6. The science test was more difficult than the history test.
7. Irene's office is bigger than Eileen's office.
8. Ronald is more capable than Donald.

Page 56 Exercise F

Listen and circle the words you hear.

1. My new chair is much more comfortable than my old chair.
2. Is that the worst city in the country?
3. I want a more energetic president.
4. Don't you have a cheaper one?
5. What was the most important day in your life?
6. Roger is the sloppiest teenager I know.
7. This is the best perfume we have.
8. Sally isn't as lazy as Richard is.
9. You know, I think your dog is meaner than mine.
10. Howard is the most honest person I know.

Page 59 Exercise G

Listen and circle the correct answer.

Ex. Ronald is younger than Fred.
1. Bob is neater than Bill.
2. The chicken is more expensive than the fish.
3. Moscow is warmer than Miami.
4. Herbert is taller than Steven.
5. Patty is more talented than Pam.

Page 63 Exercise D

Look at the map on page 62. Listen and choose the correct answer.

1. Linda was at the hotel on Ninth Avenue. She walked along Ninth Avenue to Elm Street and turned right. She walked up Elm Street to Eighth Avenue and turned right again. She went to a building on the left, between the flower shop and the post office.
2. Roger was at the shoe store on Eighth Avenue. He walked along Eighth Avenue to Oak Street and turned right. He walked down Oak Street and went to a building on the left, across from the parking garage.
3. Mr. and Mrs. Baker were at the book store on Elm Street. They walked up Elm Street to Eighth Avenue and turned right. They walked along Eighth Avenue to a building next to the pet shop and across from the post office.
4. Wanda was at the department store on Ninth Avenue. She walked along Ninth Avenue to Oak Street and turned left. She walked up Oak Street to a building on the right, next to the toy store and across from the library.
5. Alan was at the motel on Oak Street. He walked down Oak Street to Ninth Avenue and turned right. He walked along Ninth Avenue to a place on the left, next to the supermarket and across from the department store.
6. Alice was at the supermarket on Ninth Avenue. She walked along Ninth Avenue to Oak Street and turned left. She walked up Oak Street to Eighth Avenue and turned right. She went to a building on the left, across from the restaurant.

Page 67 Exercise I

Listen and fill in the correct places.

1. David took the Bay Avenue bus and got off at Second Street. He walked up Second Street to Brighton Boulevard and turned right. He walked along Brighton Boulevard to a building on the right, across from the post office. Where did he go?

2. Barbara took the Day Street bus and got off at Second Street. She walked down Second Street to Bay Avenue and turned right. She walked along Bay Avenue to a building between the flower shop and the church. Where did she go?
3. Mr. and Mrs. Jackson took the Bay Avenue bus and got off at First Street. They walked up First Street to Brighton Boulevard and turned left. They walked along Brighton Boulevard to a building on the right, next to the bus station and across from the barber shop. Where did they go?
4. Susan didn't want to take the bus this morning. She was at the library on Bay Avenue. She walked along Bay Avenue to Third Street and turned left. She walked up Third Street to Day Street and turned left again. She walked along Day Street and went to a building on the left, between First Street and Second Street. Where did she go?
5. Mr. and Mrs. Yamamoto wanted to get some exercise this morning. They took the Day Street bus and got off at First Street. They walked down First Street to Brighton Boulevard and turned left. They walked along Brighton Boulevard to Second Street and turned right. They walked down Second Street to Bay Avenue and turned right again. They went to a place on the right, at the corner of First Street and Bay Avenue, next to the concert hall. Where did they go?
6. George got lost this morning. He took the Bay Avenue bus and got off at First Street. He walked up First Street to Brighton Boulevard and turned right. He walked along Brighton Boulevard to Second Street and turned left. He walked up Second Street to Day Street and turned right. He walked along Day Street to Third Street and turned right again. He walked down Third Street to Brighton Boulevard, and then he was happy. He went to a place at the corner of Third Street and Brighton Boulevard, next to the post office and across from the pet shop. Where did he go?

Student Book Thematic Glossary

Actions and Activities

add 24
agree 47
arrive 29
ask 53
bake 13
become 32
begin 29
believe 16
bloom 32
buy 8
call 9
call in sick 36
change 46
chat online 2
chop up 24
clean 5
come 32
come home 44
communicate 8
complain 52
compliment 15
cook 3
cost 21
cut 24
dance 5
decide 23
deliver 27
disagree 47
do 5
draw 69
drink 23
drive 4
drown 35
eat 2
end 29
enjoy 25
fall 34
fall asleep 35
feel 36
fire 43
follow 68
forget 7
get back 60
get home 22
get married 29
get off 66
get out of 30
get to 33
give 6
give advice 8
go 8
go dancing 35
go hiking 2
go out 42
go outside 32

go sailing 35
go skiing 5
go swimming 35
go to bed 22
go to school 36
go to the movies 35
go to work 36
grow up 8
have 13
help 8
hire 43
hope 36
hurry 32
hurt 34
invite 69
keep 27
know 6
lend 8
like 2
listen 9
live 8
look 22
lose 8
make 12
make a list 12
make *pancakes* 4
marry 38
melt 59
miss 46
mix in 24
move 8
name 29
need 20
open 22
order 25
paint 32
pass through 59
plant 4
play 3
play baseball 32
play basketball 2
play tennis 9
play the piano 3
pour in 24
produce 27
put 24
put on 34
read 2
rebuild 59
recommend 23
rent 43
repeat 34
return 29
ride 32
rush 22
say 9

see 31
seem 44
sell 8
send 8
shop 27
sit down 22
skate 5
ski 5
slice 24
spend 16
stand 34
stay home 36
stay indoors 32
step on 35
study 42
suggest 23
swim 3
take 8
take a vacation 8
take a walk 35
take piano lessons 43
take the subway 66
talk 9
taste 17
tell 17
think 6
touch 34
try 44
turn left 64
turn right 64
visit 44
vote 42
wait 31
walk along 63
walk down 62
walk out 16
walk up 62
want 14
watch TV 2
watch videos 4
watch 34
wear 44
wonder 16
work 30
worry 35
write 3

Ailments and Symptoms

cold 32
flu 36
measles 36
nauseous 36
seasick 35
sick 35
spots 36
sunburn 35

Animals, Birds, and Insects

cat 37
dog 40
hen 27
parrot 41
puppy 33

Clothing

blouse 7
boots 32
bracelet 6
clothes 44
earrings 43
evening gown 55
gloves 43
hat 43
jacket 6
jewelry 60
necklace 6
ring 60
sweater 6
wallet 8
watch 6
winter coat 32

Colors

color 33
gray 32
green 32
pink 7
purple 7
red 36

Computers

computer 7
desktop computer 43
e-mail message 9
Internet 8
message 8
notebook computer 43
printer 41

Days of the Week 1

Sunday
Monday
Tuesday
Wednesday
Thursday
Friday
Saturday

Describing with Adjectives

afraid 35
ashamed 52
attractive 41
bad 15

baked 25
beautiful 41
best 54
better 44
big 28
boring 51
bright 50
broiled 25
busy 27
capable 43
careful 34
cheap 42
clean 45
clear 60
close 60
cold 31
comfortable 41
concerned 53
convenient 43
cute 39
delicious 15
dependable 56
different 27
difficult 27
direct 66
disappointed 22
dishonest 59
easy 44
elegant 55
embarrassed 52
energetic 49
enormous 27
excellent 15
exciting 39
expensive 21
famous 31
fancy 40
fantastic 15
fashionable 39
fast 40
favorite 24
first 25
fresh 13
friendly 39
funny 49
fur 43
generous 49
glad 15
good 8
handsome 41
happy 31
hard 44
healthy 44
helpful 49
high 59
honest 42
horrible 52
hospitable 39
hot 39
hungry 22

impatient 59
impolite 59
inexpensive 59
intelligent 39
interesting 41
kind 50
large 27
last 4
late 22
lazy 39
leather 43
left 43
light 28
lightweight 55
little 27
long 27
lost 68
low 27
magnificent 23
mean 49
modern 47
neat 44
new 8
nice 41
noisy 49
obnoxious 49
old 40
out of this world 23
outdoor 60
patient 49
polite 39
popular 49
positive 35
powerful 39
pregnant 36
pretty 40
proud 52
quick 66
quiet 25
ready 30
real 46
reasonable 57
reliable 46
ridiculous 45
right 43
romantic 25
rude 49
sad 32
safe 40
satisfied 44
short 44
sick 9
sloppy 49
small 27
smart 39
soft 39
special 24
spicy 39
stubborn 49
stupid 68

sure 35
sympathetic 44
talented 39
talkative 39
tall 47
tasty 25
terrible 17
tired 22
ugly 52
uncomfortable 59
understanding 44
unfriendly 59
unhealthy 59
unsafe 59
upset 16
used 42
useful 42
wide 47
wonderful 15
worse 56
worst 56
wrong 68

Describing with Adverbs

always 8
completely 68
never 8
often 8
soon 24
usually 28

Entertainment and the Arts

entertainment 60
jazz 5
movie 43
music 44
piano lesson 43
radio talk show 46
rock music 5
TV program 58

Events and Occurrences

anniversary 7
birthday 6
blackout 84
celebration 59
costume party 59
date 25
party 24
picnic 35
vacation 33
wedding anniversary 25

Family Members

aunt 50
brother 30
children 7
cousin 50

daughter 6
family 5
father 4
grandchildren 7
grandfather 51
grandmother 2
husband 6
mother 32
nephew 51
parent 7
sister 50
son 44
uncle 50
wife 6

Food Containers and Quantities

bag 19
bottle 19
bowl 23
box 19
bunch 19
can 19
cup 23
dish 23
dozen 19
gallon 19
glass 23
half a pound 19
half pound 19
head 19
jar 19
loaf 19
order 23
piece 23
pint 19
pound 19
quart 19
slice 27

Foods

appetizer 25
apple pie 13
apple 11
bagel 27
baked chicken 25
baking soda 24
banana 11
bread 11
broiled fish 25
butter 12
cake 11
candy 6
carrot 11
cereal 19
cheese 8
chicken 11
chicken soup 23
chili 27
chocolate bar 27
chocolate cake 15

landlord 50
mayor 46
professor 43
senator 51
singer 58
teacher 24
TV star 58
waiter 25
waitress 25

Parts of the Body

arm 36
eyes 34
feet 35
hair 44
hand 43
head 34
leg 35

People

boss 45
boy 32
girl 52
guest 30
neighbor 51
people 31
person 50
salespeople 56
student 53
teenager 44
worker 59

Places Around Town

airport 61
amusement park 60
apartment building 41
bakery 28
bank 70
barber shop 62
baseball stadium 61
beach 2
book store 64
bus station 64
bus stop 68
cafeteria 64
church 8
city 47
clinic 62
college 8
concert hall 61
courthouse 61
department store 56
drug store 62
fire station 64
flower shop 61
food store 27
gas station 63
grocery store 27

hardware store 61
high school 8
hospital 8
hotel 59
ice cream shop 61
laundromat 62
library 62
mall 2
motel 61
museum 61
neighborhood 31
office 36
open market 27
park 32
parking garage 61
parking lot 63
pet shop 61
place 27
playground 61
police station 62
post office 62
restaurant 25
school 33
shoe store 61
shopping mall 64
station 59
subway station 59
subway 59
supermarket 16
tourist sight 58
town 56
toy store 61
train station 66
university 61
wholesale store 27
zoo 63

School

class 68
course 43
English class 68
grades 44
history professor 51
student 53
test 31

Seasons 1

spring
summer
fall/autumn
winter

Sports and Recreation

camping 60
football 60
fun 60
game 30
recreation 60

soccer 60
sport 58
sports equipment 60
swimming pool 59
tennis racket 40
walk 32

Time Expressions

a minute 24
all the time 17
all *year* 32
at *7:00* 30
day 1
early in the *evening* 28
evening 25
every day 3
every *morning* 36
for *45* minutes 24
for a long time 27
for *three* hours 24
hour 24
in a few hours 30
in a few minutes 30
in a few more *weeks* 32
in a little while 30
in a week 30
in an hour 30
in *five* minutes 30
in half an hour 30
in the past 27
in *two* or *three* days 30
last January/February/
    . . ./December 4
last night 4
last spring/summer/fall
    (autumn)/winter 4
last Sunday/Monday/
    . . ./Saturday 4
last week/weekend/
    month/year 4
month 1
next *Saturday* 33
now 8
on *Sunday* afternoons
    32
on the weekend 2
once or twice a week 27
right now 3
season 1
some day 31
the middle of the
    afternoon 28
these days 27
this January/February/
    . . ./December 5
this morning/afternoon/
    evening 4

this spring/summer/fall
    (autumn)/winter 4
this Sunday/Monday/
    . . ./Saturday 5
this week/weekend/
    month/year 4
time 27
today 4
tomorrow 3
tomorrow morning/
    afternoon/evening/
    night 9
tonight 5
two years ago 6
week 27
weekend 2
year 1
yesterday 3
yesterday morning/
    afternoon/evening 4

Transportation

bus 66
bus system 46
car 42
motorcycle 42
sports car 40
train 30
van 8
wheel 59

Weather

cold 32
cool 47
hot 47
rain 31
rainy 47
snow 32
snowy 47
storm 30
sunny 32
warm 32
weather 32

Work

boss 45
company 27
company picnic 35
helmet 29
job 8
machine 34
office 36
safety glasses 29
work 22

Cardinal Numbers

1	one	20	twenty
2	two	21	twenty-one
3	three	22	twenty-two
4	four	.	.
5	five	.	.
6	six	29	twenty-nine
7	seven	30	thirty
8	eight	40	forty
9	nine	50	fifty
10	ten	60	sixty
11	eleven	70	seventy
12	twelve	80	eighty
13	thirteen	90	ninety
14	fourteen		
15	fifteen	100	one hundred
16	sixteen	200	two hundred
17	seventeen	300	three hundred
18	eighteen	.	.
19	nineteen	.	.
		900	nine hundred
		1,000	one thousand
		2,000	two thousand
		3,000	three thousand
		.	.
		10,000	ten thousand
		100,000	one hundred thousand
		1,000,000	one million

Ordinal Numbers

1st	first	20th	twentieth
2nd	second	21st	twenty-first
3rd	third	22nd	twenty-second
4th	fourth	.	.
5th	fifth	.	.
6th	sixth	29th	twenty-ninth
7th	seventh	30th	thirtieth
8th	eighth	40th	fortieth
9th	ninth	50th	fiftieth
10th	tenth	60th	sixtieth
11th	eleventh	70th	seventieth
12th	twelfth	80th	eightieth
13th	thirteenth	90th	ninetieth
14th	fourteenth		
15th	fifteenth	100th	one hundredth
16th	sixteenth	1,000th	one thousandth
17th	seventeenth	1,000,000th	one millionth
18th	eighteenth		
19th	nineteenth		

How to Read a Date

June 9, 1941 = "June ninth, nineteen forty-one"

November 16, 2010 = "November sixteenth, two thousand ten" *or*
"November sixteenth, two thousand and ten"

Irregular Verbs: Past Tense

be	was	lead	led
become	became	leave	left
begin	began	lend	lent
bite	bit	lose	lost
break	broke	make	made
build	built	meet	met
buy	bought	put	put
catch	caught	read	read
come	came	ride	rode
cost	cost	run	ran
cut	cut	say	said
do	did	see	saw
drink	drank	sell	sold
drive	drove	send	sent
eat	ate	shake	shook
fall	fell	sing	sang
feed	fed	sit	sat
feel	felt	sleep	slept
find	found	speak	spoke
fly	flew	spend	spent
forget	forgot	stand	stood
get	got	steal	stole
give	gave	swim	swam
go	went	take	took
grow	grew	teach	taught
have	had	tell	told
hear	heard	think	thought
hurt	hurt	understand	understood
keep	kept	wear	wore
know	knew	write	wrote

Index

A

Adjectives, 15, 25, 39-47, 49–59
A few, 14–16, 24
A little, 14–16, 24
Any, 13
As + adjective + as, 45–47

C

Comparative of adjectives, 40–47,
   54–55, 57
Could/couldn't, 34, 65
Count/non-count nouns, 12–17,
   22–25

D

Dates, 7
Days of the week, 1, 4–5
Directions, 62–69

F

Foods, 11–17, 19–25, 27
Future: going to, 3–6, 33
Future: will, 30–32, 35–37

I

Indirect object pronouns, 6–9
Imperatives, 23–24, 34

L

Like to, 2–5
Like vs. like to, 5

M

Many, 14–15, 17
Might, 33–37
Months, 1, 4–5, 7
Much, 14–15, 17, 21

P

Partitives, 20–23, 25
Places around town, 61–69
Possessive pronouns, 45
Prepositions of location, 62–67
Present continuous tense, 3
Pronouns:
   Indirect object, 6–9
   Possessive, 45

Q

Quantity
   A few, 14–16, 24
   A little, 14–16, 24
   Many, 14–15, 17
   Much, 14–15, 17

S

Seasons, 1, 4–5
Should, 42–44
Simple past tense, 3–7, 22, 25, 68
Simple present tense, 3, 8, 17,
   56–57
Superlatives, 50–59

T

Tenses:
   Future: going to, 3–6, 33
   Future: will, 30–32, 35–37
   Review of tenses, 3–5
   Simple past, 3–7, 22, 25, 68
Time expressions, 4–6, 30

W

Would, 15, 23, 35, 64

Correlation Key

Student Book Pages	Activity Workbook Pages	Student Book Pages	Activity Workbook Pages
Chapter 1		**Chapter 5**	
2	2	40	40
3	3	41	41–42
4–5	4–7	42–43	43–46
6	8	45	47–49
7	9–11	47	50
Chapter 2		**Chapter 6**	
12	12–13	50	51
13	14–15	51	52–54
14	16–17	54–55	55–57
15	18–20	**Check-Up Test**	58–59
Chapter 3		**Gazette**	59a–d
20	21–23	**Chapter 7**	
21	24	62	60
23	25–26	63	61
24	27	64–65	62–64
Check-Up Test	28–29	66	65–66
Gazette	29a–b	67	67
Chapter 4			
30	30		
31	31–33		
33	34		
34	35		
35	36–39		

SIDE *by* SIDE *Extra* Activity Workbook Audio Program

The *Side by Side Extra* Activity Workbook Digital Audio CD contains all Workbook listening activities and GrammarRaps and GrammarSongs for entertaining language practice through rhythm and music. Students can use the Audio Program to extend their language learning through self-study outside the classroom. The Digital Audio CD also includes MP3 files of the audio program for downloading to a computer or audio player.

Audio Program Contents